CSS

Pocket Reference

SECOND EDITION

CSS

Pocket Reference

Eric A. Meyer

O'REILLY®

Beijing · Cambridge · Farnham · Köln · Paris · Sebastopol · Taipei · Tokyo

SHROFF PUBLISHERS & DISTRIBUTORS PVT. LTD.
Mumbai Bangalore Chennai Kolkata New Delhi

CSS Pocket Reference, Second Edition

by Eric A. Meyer

Originally printed in the United States of America. ISBN: 0-596-00777-9

Published by O'Reilly Media Inc., 1005 Gravenstein Highway North, Sebastopol, CA 95472.

O'Reilly books may be purchased for educational, business, or sales promotional use. Online editions are also available for most titles (*safari.oreilly.com*). For more information, contact our corporate/institutional sales department: (800) 998-9938 or *corporate@oreilly.com*.

Editor: Molly Wood and Tatiana Apandi Diaz

Production Editor: Colleen Gorman

Cover Designer: Ellie Volckhausen

Interior Designer: Melanie Wang

Printing History:

May 2001: First Edition.
July 2004: Second Edition.

First Indian Reprint: February 2007

ISBN 10: 81-8404-265-5
ISBN 13: 978-81-8404-265-8

Published by **Shroff Publishers and Distributors Pvt. Ltd.** C-103, MIDC, TTC Industrial Area, Pawane, Navi Mumbai 400 701, Tel: (91 22) 2763 4290, Fax: (91 22) 2768 3337, e-mail: spdorders@shroffpublishers.com. Printed at Rose Fine Art, Mumbai.

Contents

CSS Pocket Reference

Cascading Style Sheets (CSS) is the W3C standard for the visual presentation of web pages (although it can be used in other settings as well). After a short introduction to the key concepts of CSS, this pocket reference provides an alphabetical reference to all CSS2.1 selectors, followed by an alphabetical reference for all CSS2.1 properties.

Conventions Used in This Book

The following typographical conventions are used in this book:

Italic

Used to indicate new terms, URLs, filenames, file extensions, directories, commands and options, and program names. For example, a path in the filesystem will appear as *C:\windows\system*.

`Constant width`

Used to show the contents of files or the output from commands.

For more information, visit O'Reilly's web site for this book, where examples, errata, and any plans for future editions are listed:

http://www.oreilly.com/catalog/csspr2

Adding Styles to HTML and XHTML

Styles can be applied to documents in three distinct ways, as discussed in the following sections.

Inline Styles

In HTML and XHTML, style information can be specified for an individual element via the `style` attribute. The value of a `style` attribute is a declaration block without the curly brackets.

```
<p style="color: red; background: yellow;">Look out!
This text is alarmingly presented!</p>
```

Note that, as of this writing, a full style sheet cannot be placed into a style attribute. For example, it is not possible to place hover styles (using `:hover`) in a `style` attribute.

Although typical XML document languages (e.g., XHTML 1. 0, XHTML 1.1, and SVG) support the `style` attribute, it is unlikely that all XML languages will support a similar capability. Due to this and the fact that it encourages poor authoring practices, authors are generally discouraged from using the `style` attribute.

Embedded Style Sheets

A style sheet can be embedded at the top of an HTML or XHTML document using the `style` element, which must appear within the head element.

```
<html><head><title>Stylin'!</title>
<style type="text/css">
h1 {color: purple;}
p {font-size: smaller; color: gray;}
</style>
</head>
   ...
</html>
```

XML languages may or may not provide an equivalent capability; always check the language DTD to be certain.

External Style Sheets

Styles can be listed in a separate file. The primary advantage to a separate file is that by collecting commonly used styles in a single file, all pages that use that style sheet can be updated by editing a single style sheet. Another key advantage is that external style sheets are cached, which can help reduce bandwidth usage. An external style sheet can be referenced in one of the following three ways.

@import directive

One or more `@import` directives can be placed at the beginning of any style sheet. Inside an HTML and XHTML document, this would be done within an embedded style sheet.

```
<head>
<title>My Document</title>
<style type="text/css">
@import url(site.css);
@import url(navbar.css);
@import url(footer.css);
body {background: yellow;}
</style>
</head>
```

Note that `@import` directives can appear at the top of any style sheet. Thus, one style sheet could import another, which in turn imports a third.

link element

In HTML and XHTML documents, the `link` element can be used to associate a style sheet with the document. Multiple `link` elements are permitted. The `media` attribute can be used to restrict a style sheet to one or more media.

```
<head>
<title>A Document</title>
<link rel="stylesheet" type="text/css" href="basic.css"
```

```
  media="all">
<link rel="stylesheet" type="text/css" href="web.css"
  media="screen">
<link rel="stylesheet" type="text/css" href="paper.css"
  media="print">
</head>
```

It is also possible to link to alternate style sheets. If alternate style sheets are supplied, it is up to the user agent (or the author) to provide a means for the user to select one of the alternates.

```
<head>
<title>A Document</title>
<link rel="stylesheet" type="text/css" href="basic.css">
<link rel="alternate stylesheet" title="Classic"
type="text/css" href="oldschool.css">
<link rel="alternate stylesheet" title="Futuristic"
type="text/css" href="3000ad.css">
</head>
```

As of this writing, most or all known user agents load all linked style sheets, including the alternate style sheets, regardless of whether the user ever uses them. This can have implications for bandwidth use and server load.

xml-stylesheet processing instruction

In XML documents (such as XHTML documents sent with a mime-type of "text/xml", "application/xml", or "application/xhtml+xml"), the `xml-stylesheet` processing instruction can be used to associate a style sheet with the document. Any `xml-stylesheet` processing instructions must be placed in the prolog of an XML document. Multiple `xml-stylesheet` processing instructions are permitted. The `media` pseudo-attribue can be used to restrict a style sheet to one or more forms of media.

```
<?xml-stylesheet type="text/css" href="basic.css"
  media="all"?>
<?xml-stylesheet type="text/css" href="web.css"
  media="screen"?>
<?xml-stylesheet type="text/css" href="paper.css"
  media="print"?>
```

It is also possible to link to alternate style sheets with the `xml-stylesheet` processing instruction

```
<?xml-stylesheet type="text/css" href="basic.css"?>
<?xml-stylesheet alternate="yes" title="Classic"
  type="text/css" href="oldschool.css"?>
<?xml-stylesheet alternate="yes" title="Futuristic"
  type="text/css" href="3000ad.css"?>
```

Rule Structure

A style sheet consists of one of more rules that describe how page elements should be presented. Every rule has two fundamental parts: the *selector* and the *declaration block*. Figure 1 illustrates the structure of a rule.

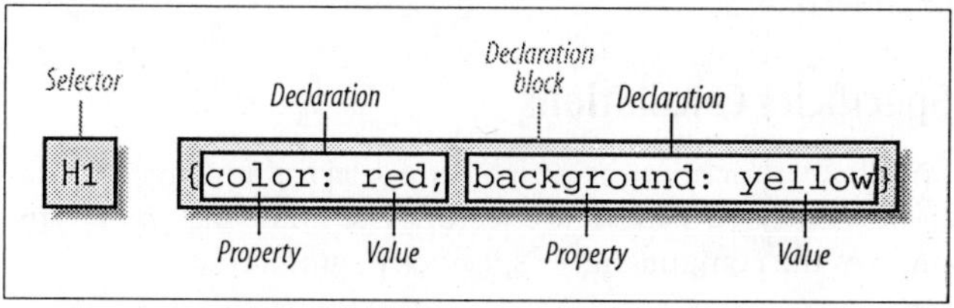

Figure 1. Rule structure

On the left side of the rule, we find the selector, which selects the parts of the document to which the rule should be applied. On the right side of the rule, we have the declaration block. A declaration block is made up of one or more *declarations*; each declaration is a combination of a CSS *property* and a *value* of that property.

The declaration block is always enclosed in curly brackets. A declaration block can contain several declarations; each declaration must be terminated with a semicolon (;). The exception is the final declaration in a declaration block, for which the semicolon is optional.

Each property, which represents a particular stylistic parameter, is separated from its value by a colon (:). Property names in CSS are not case-sensitive. Legal values for a property are defined by the property description. The "Property Reference" section, later in this book, provides details on acceptable values for CSS properties.

Style Precedence

A single HTML document can import and link to multiple external style sheets, contain one or more embedded style sheets, and make use of inline styles. In the process, it is quite possible that some rules will conflict with each other. CSS uses a mechanism called the *cascade* to resolve any such conflicts and arrive at a final set of styles to be applied to the document. Two key components of the cascade are *specificity* and *inheritance*.

Specificity Calculations

Specificity describes the weight of a selector and any declarations associated with that selector. The following chart summarizes the components of specificity summation.

Selector type	Specificity
Universal selector Combinators	`0,0,0,0`
Element identifier Pseudo-element identifier	`0,0,0,1`
Class identifier Pseudo-class identifier Attribute identifier	`0,0,1,0`
ID identifier	`0,1,0,0`
Inline style	`1,0,0,0`

Specificity values are cumulative. Thus, a selector containing two element identifiers and a class identifier (e.g., `div.aside p`) has a specificity of 0,0,1,2. Specificity values are sorted in right-to-left precedence; thus, a selector containing eleven element identifiers (0,0,0,11) is of lower specificity than a selector containing just a single class identifier (0,0,1,0).

The `!important` directive gives a declaration more weight than nonimportant declarations. The declaration retains the specificity of its selectors, and is used only in comparison with other important declarations.

Inheritance

The elements in a document form a tree-like hierarchy with the root element at the top and the rest of the document structure spreading out below it (which makes it look more like a tree root system, really). In an HTML document, the `html` element is at the top of the tree, with the `head` and `body` elements descending from it. From those elements descend the rest of the document structure. In such a structure, elements lower down in the tree are descendants of the ancestors, which are higher in the tree.

CSS uses the document tree for the mechanism of *inheritance*, in which a style applied to an element is inherited by its descendants. For example, if the `body` element is set to have a `color` of `red`, that value propagates down the document tree to the elements that descend from the `body` element. This inheritance is interrupted only by a style rule that applies directly to an element. Inherited values have no specificity at all (which is *not* the same as having zero specificity).

Note that some elements are not inherited. A property will always define whether it is inherited. Some examples of noninherited properties are `padding`, `border`, `margin`, and `background`.

The Cascade

The cascade is how CSS resolves conflicts between styles; it is, in other words, the mechanism by which a user agent decides, for example, what color to make an element when two different rules apply to it and each one tries to set a different color. The following steps constitute the cascade:

1. Find all declarations that contain a selector that matches a given element.
2. Sort by explicit weight all declarations applying to the element. Those rules marked `!important` are given greater weight than those that are not. Also, sort by origin all declarations applying to a given element. There are three origins: author, reader, and user agent. Under normal circumstances, the author's styles win out over the reader's styles. `!important` reader styles are stronger than any other styles, including `!important` author styles. Both author and reader styles override the user agent's default styles.
3. Sort by specificity all declarations applying to a given element. Those elements with a higher specificity have more weight than those with lower specificity.
4. Sort by order all declarations applying to a given element. The later a declaration appears in the style sheet or document, the more weight it is given. Declarations that appear in an imported style sheet are considered to come before all declarations within the style sheet that imports them.

Element Classification

Broadly speaking, CSS groups elements into two types: *replaced* and *nonreplaced*. Although the types may seem rather abstract, there actually are some differences in how the two kinds of element are presented. These differences are explored in detail in Chapter 7 of *Cascading Style Sheets: The Definitive Guide*, Second Edition (O'Reilly).

Nonreplaced Elements

The majority of HTML and XHTML elements are *nonreplaced elements*. This means their content is presented by the user agent inside a box generated by the element itself. For example, `<span>hi there</span>` is a nonreplaced element, and the text `hi there` will be displayed by the user agent. Paragraphs, headings, table cells, lists, and almost everything else in XHTML are nonreplaced elements.

Replaced Elements

In contrast, *replaced elements* are those where the element's content is replaced by something not directly represented by document content. The most familiar XHTML example is the `img` element, which is replaced by an image file external to the document itself. In fact, `img` has no actual content, as we can see by considering a simple example.

```
<img src="howdy.gif" alt="Hi" />
```

There is no content contained in the element—only an element name and attributes. Only by replacing the element's lack of content with content found through other means (in this case, loading an external image specified by the `src` attribute) can the element have any presentation at all. Another example is the `input` element, which may be replaced with a radio button, checkbox, or text input box, depending on its type. Replaced elements also generate boxes in their display.

Element Display Roles

In addition to being replaced or not, there are two basic types of element display roles in CSS2: *block-level* and *inline-level*.

Block-Level

Block-level elements are those that generate an element box that (by default) fills its parent element's content area, and cannot have other elements to its sides. In other words, block-level elements generate "breaks" before and after the element box. The most familiar block elements from HTML are `p` and `div`. Replaced elements can be block-level elements, but usually are not.

List items are a special case of block-level elements. In addition to behaving in a manner consistent with other block elements, they generate a marker—typically a bullet for unordered lists or a number for ordered lists—which is "attached" to the element box. Except for the presence of this marker, list items are in all other ways identical to other block elements.

Inline-Level Elements

Inline-level elements are those that generate an element box within a line of text and do not break up the flow of that line. The best inline element example is the a element in XHTML. Other candidates would be `strong` and `em`. These elements do not generate a break before or after themselves and so can appear within the content of another element without disrupting its display.

Note that while the CSS block and inline elements have a great deal in common with HTML and XHTML block- and inline-level elements, there is an important difference: in HTML and XHTML, block-level elements cannot descend from inline-level elements, whereas in CSS, there is no restriction on how display roles can be nested within each other.

Basic Visual Layout

CSS defines algorithms for laying out any element in a document. These algorithms form the underpinnings of visual presentation in CSS. There are two primary kinds of layout, each with very different behaviors: block-level and inline-level layout.

Block-Level Layout

A block-level box in CSS generates a rectangular box called the *element box*. This box describes the amount of space occupied by an element. Figure 2 shows the various components of an element box. The following rules apply to an element box:

- The background of an element extends to the outer edge of the border, thus filling the content, padding, and border areas. If the border has any transparent portions (e.g, it is dotted or dashed), then the background will be visible in those portions.
- Only the margins, `height`, and `width` of an element box may be set to `auto`.
- Only margins can be given negative length values.
- The padding and borders of the element box default to `0` (zero) and `none`, respectively.
- The property `width` defines only the width of the content area; any padding, borders, or margins are added to it. The same is true for `height`.

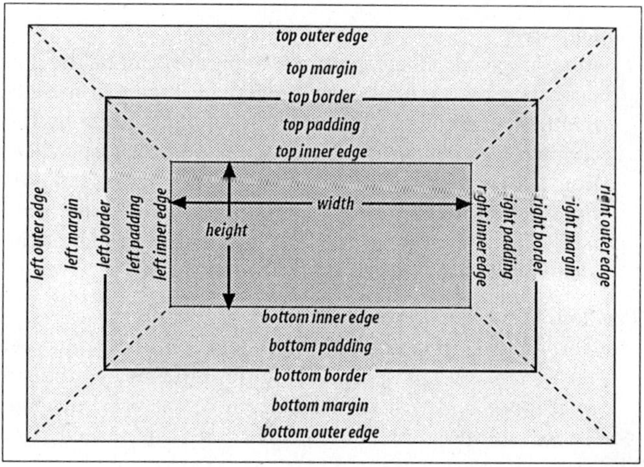

Figure 2. Box model details

Inline Layout

All inline elements have a `line-height`, which has a great deal to do with how the elements are displayed. The height of a line of text is determined by taking into account the following factors:

Anonymous text
: Any string of characters not contained within an inline element. Thus, in the markup:

```
<p> I'm <em>so</em> happy!</p>
```

the sequences " I'm " and " happy!" are anonymous text. Note that the spaces are part of that text, since a space is a character like any other.

Em-box
: The em-box defined in the given font; otherwise known as the character box. Actual glyphs can be taller or shorter than their em-boxes, as discussed in Chapter 5 of *Cascading Style Sheets: The Definitive Guide*, Second Edition. In CSS, the value of `font-size` determines the height of each em-box.

Content area
: In nonreplaced elements, the content area can be the box described by the em-boxes of every character in the element, strung together, or else the box described by the character glyphs in the element. The CSS2.1 specification allows user agents to choose either. This text uses the em-box definition, for simplicity's sake. In replaced elements, the content area is the intrinsic height of the element plus any margins, borders, or padding.

Leading
: The leading is the difference between the values of `font-size` and `line-height`. Half this difference is applied to the top and half to the bottom of the content area. These additions to the content area are called, not

surprisingly, half-leading. Leading is applied only to non-replaced elements.

Inline box

The box described by the addition of the leading to the content area. For nonreplaced elements, the height of the inline box of an element will be equal to the value for `line-height`. For replaced elements, the height of the inline box of an element will be equal to the content area, since leading is not applied to replaced elements.

Line box

The shortest box that bounds the highest and lowest points of the inline boxes that are found in the line. In other words, the top edge of the line box will be placed along the top of the highest inline box top, and the bottom of the line box is placed along the bottom of the lowest inline box bottom. (See Figure 3.)

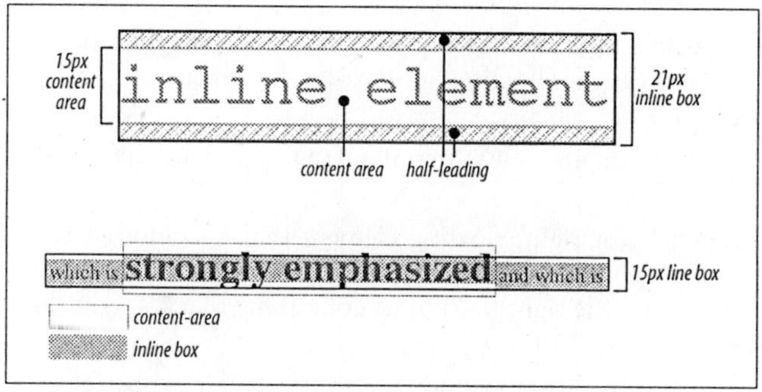

Figure 3. Inline layout details

Floating Rules

Floating allows an element to be placed to the left or right of its containing block (which is the nearest block-level ancestor element), with following content flowing around the element. A floated element is placed according to the following rules:

1. The left (or right) outer edge of a floated element may not be to the left (or right) of the inner edge of its containing block.
2. The left (or right) outer edge of a floated element must be to the right (or left) of the right (left) outer edge of a left-floating (or right-floating) element that occurs earlier in the document's source, unless the top of the later element is below the bottom of the former.
3. The right outer edge of a left-floating element may not be to the right of the left outer edge of any right-floating element to its right. The left outer edge of a right-floating element may not be to the left of the right outer edge of any left-floating element to its left.
4. A floating element's top may not be higher than the inner top of its containing block.
5. A floating element's top may not be higher than the top of any earlier floating or block-level element.
6. A floating element's top may not be higher than the top of any line box with content that precedes the floating element.
7. A left (or right) floating element that has another floating element to its left (right) may not have its right outer edge to the right (left) of its containing block's right (left) edge.
8. A floating element must be placed as high as possible.
9. A left-floating element must be put as far to the left as possible, a right-floating element as far to the right as possible. A higher position is preferred to one that is further to the right or left.

Positioning Rules

When elements are positioned, a number of special rules come into play. These rules govern not only the containing block of the element, but also how it is laid out within that element.

Types of Positioning

Static positioning
: The element's box is generated as normal. Block-level elements generate a rectangular box that is part of the document's flow, and inline-level boxes generate one or more line boxes that flow within their parent element.

Relative positioning
: The element's box is offset by some distance. Its containing block can be considered to be the area that the element would occupy if it were not positioned. The element retains the shape it would have had were it not positioned, and the space that the element would ordinarily have occupied is preserved.

Absolute positioning
: The element's box is completely removed from the flow of the document and positioned with respect to its containing block, which may be another element in the document or the initial containing block (described in the next section). Whatever space the element might have occupied in the normal document flow is closed up, as though the element did not exist. The positioned element generates a block box, regardless of the type of box it would generate if it were in the normal flow.

Fixed positioning
: The element's box behaves as though it were set to `absolute`, but its containing block is the viewport itself.

The Containing Block

The containing block of a positioned element is determined as follows:

1. The containing block of the *root element* (also called the *initial containing block*) is established by the user agent. In HTML, the root element is the `html` element, although some browsers may use `body`.
2. For nonroot elements, if the element's `position` value is `relative` or `static`, the containing block is formed by the content edge of the nearest block-level, table-, cell-, or inline-block ancestor box. (Despite this rule, relatively positioned elements are still simply offset, not positioned with respect to the containing block described here.)
3. For nonroot elements that have a `position` value of `absolute`, the containing block is set to the nearest ancestor (of any kind) that has a `position` value other than `static`. This happens as follows:
   a. If the ancestor is block-level, the containing block is that element's padding edge; in other words, it is the area that would be bounded by a border.
   b. If the ancestor is inline-level, the containing block is set to the content edge of the ancestor. In left-to-right languages, the top and left of the containing block are the top and left content edges of the first box in the ancestor, and the bottom and right edges are the bottom and right content edges of the last box. In right-to-left languages, the right edge of the containing block corresponds to the right content edge of the first box, and the left is taken from the last box. The top and bottom are the same.
   c. If there are no ancestors as described in a) and b), then the element's containing block is defined to be the initial containing block.

Layout of Absolutely Positioned Elements

In the following sections, these terms are used:

Shrink-to-fit
: Similar to calculating the width of a table cell using the automatic table layout algorithm. In general, the user agent attempts to find the minimum element width that will contain the content and will wrap to multiple lines only if wrapping cannot be avoided.

Static position
: The place where an element's edge would have been placed if its `position` were `static`.

Horizontal layout of nonreplaced absolutely positioned elements

The equation that governs the layout of these elements is:

```
left + margin-left + border-left-width + padding-left +
width + padding-right + border-right-width + margin-right
+ right = width of containing block
```

The steps used to determine layout are:

1. If all of `left`, `width`, and `right` are `auto`, first reset any `auto` values for `margin-left` and `margin-right` to `0`. Then, if `direction` is `ltr`, set `left` to the static position and apply the third rule in the list given in step 3. Otherwise, set `right` to the static position and apply the first rule in the list given in step 3.
2. If none of `left`, `width`, and `right` are `auto`, pick the rule that applies from the following list:
   a. If both `margin-left` and `margin-right` are set to `auto`, solve the equation under the additional constraint that the two margins get equal values.
   b. If only one of `margin-left` or `margin-right` is set to `auto`, solve the equation for that value.

   c. If the values are overconstrained (none are set to auto), ignore the value for left (if direction is rtl; ignore right if direction is ltr) and solve for that value.

3. If some of left, width, and right are auto, but others are not, reset any auto values for margin-left and margin-right to 0. From the following list, pick the one rule that applies:
   a. If left and width are auto and right is not auto, then the width is shrink-to-fit. Solve the equation for left.
   b. If left and right are auto and width is not auto, then if direction is ltr, set left to the static position (otherwise, set right to the static position). Solve the equation for left (if direction is rtl) or right (if direction is ltr).
   c. If width and right are auto and left is not auto, then the width is shrink-to-fit. Solve the question for right.
   d. If left is auto, and width and right are not auto, solve the equation for left.
   e. If width is auto, and left and right are not auto, solve the equation for width.
   f. If right is auto, and left and width are not auto, solve the equation for right.

Vertical layout of nonreplaced absolutely positioned elements

The equation that governs the layout of these elements is:

```
top + margin-top + border-top-width + padding-top + height
+ padding-bottom + border-bottom-width + margin-bottom +
bottom = height of containing block
```

The steps used to determine layout are:

1. If all of top, height, and bottom are auto, set top to the static position and apply the third rule in the list given in step 3.

2. If none of top, height, and bottom are auto, pick the one rule that applies from the following list:
   a. If both margin-top and margin-bottom are set to auto, solve the equation under the additional constraint that the two margins get equal values.
   b. If only one of margin-top or margin-bottom is set to auto, solve the equation for that value.
   c. If the values are overconstrained (none are set to auto), ignore the value for bottom and solve for that value.
3. If some of top, height, and bottom are auto, but others are not, pick the one rule that applies from the following list:
   a. If top and height are auto and bottom is not auto, then the height is based on the element's content (as it would be in the static flow). Reset any auto values for margin-top and margin-bottom to 0 and solve the equation for top.
   b. If top and bottom are auto and height is not auto, then set top to the static position. Reset any auto values for margin-top and margin-bottom to 0 and solve the equation for bottom.
   c. If height and bottom are auto and top is not auto, then the height is based on the element's content (as it would be in the static flow). Reset any auto values for margin-top and margin-bottom to 0 and solve the equation for bottom.
   d. If top is auto, and height and bottom are not auto, reset any auto values for margin-top and margin-bottom to 0 and solve the equation for top.
   e. If height is auto, and top and bottom are not auto, reset any auto values for margin-top and margin-bottom to 0 and solve the equation for height.
   f. If bottom is auto, and top and height are not auto, reset any auto values for margin-top and margin-bottom to 0 and solve the equation for bottom.

Horizontal layout of replaced absolutely positioned elements

The behaviors that go into placing and sizing replaced elements are most easily expressed as a series of rules to be taken one after the other. These rules state:

1. If `width` is set to `auto`, the computed value of `width` is determined by the intrinsic width of the element's content. Thus, the width of an image 50 pixels wide is computed to be `50px`. If `width` is explicitly declared (that is, something like `100px` or `50%`), then the width is set to that value.
2. If `left` has the value `auto` in a left-to-right language, replace `auto` with the static position. In right-to-left languages, replace an `auto` value for `right` with the static position.
3. If either `left` or `right` is still `auto` (in other words, it hasn't been replaced in a previous step), replace any `auto` value in `margin-left` or `margin-right` with `0`.
4. If at this point both `margin-left` and `margin-right` are still defined to be `auto`, set them to be equal, thus centering the element in its containing block.
5. After all that, if there is only one `auto` value left, change it to equal the remainder of the equation.

Vertical layout of replaced absolutely positioned elements

The behaviors that go into placing and sizing replaced elements are most easily expressed as a series of rules to be taken one after the other. These state:

1. If `height` is set to `auto`, the computed value of `height` is determined by the intrinsic height of the element's content. Thus, the height of an image 50 pixels tall is computed to be `50px`. If `height` is explicitly declared (that is, something like `100px` or `50%`), then the height is set to that value.

2. If `top` has the value `auto`, replace the value with the replaced element's static position.
3. If `bottom` has a value of `auto`, replace any `auto` value on `margin-top` or `margin-bottom` with `0`.
4. If at this point both `margin-top` and `margin-bottom` are still defined to be `auto`, set them to be equal, thus centering the element in its containing block.
5. After all that, if there is only one `auto` value left, change it to equal the remainder of the equation.

Table Layout

The layout of tables can get quite complicated, especially since CSS defines two different ways to calculate table and cell widths, as well as two ways to handle the borders of tables and elements internal to the table. Figure 4 illustrates the components of a table.

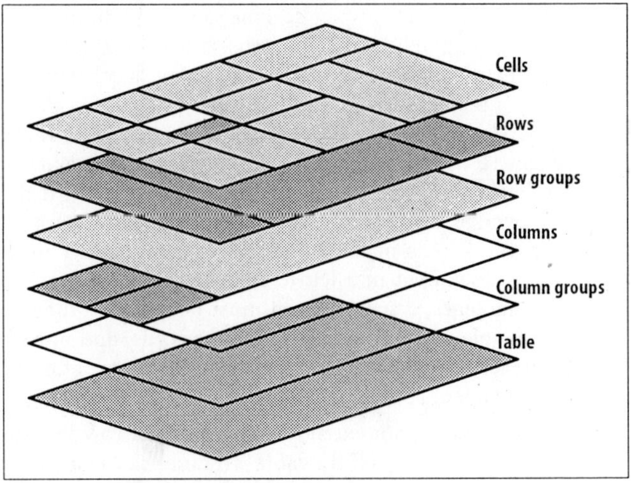

Figure 4. Table layout components

Table Arrangement Rules

In general, a table is laid out according to the following principles:

1. Each row box encompasses a single row of grid cells. All of the row boxes in a table fill the table from top to bottom in the order they occur in the source document. Thus, the table contains as many grid rows as there are row elements.
2. A row group's box encompasses the same grid cells as the row boxes that it contains.
3. A column box encompasses one or more columns of grid cells. Column boxes are placed next to each other in the order they occur. The first column box is on the left for left-to-right languages and on the right for right-to-left languages.
4. A column group's box encompasses the same grid cells as the column boxes that it contains.
5. Although cells may span several rows or columns, CSS does not define how this happens. It is instead left to the document language to define spanning. Each spanned cell is a rectangular box one or more grid cells wide and high. The top row of this rectangle is in the row that is parent to the cell. The cell's rectangle must be as far to the left as possible in left-to-right languages, but it may not overlap any other cell box. It must also be to the right of all cells in the same row that are earlier in the source document in a left-to-right language. In right-to-left languages, a spanned cell must be as far to the right as possible without overlapping other cells, and must be to the left of all cells in the same row that come after it in the document source.
6. A cell's box cannot extend beyond the last row box of a table or row group. If the table structure causes this condition, the cell must be shortened until it fits within the table or row group that encloses it.

Fixed Table Layout

The fixed-layout model is fast because its layout doesn't depend on the contents of table cells; it's driven by the `width` values of the table, columns and cells within the first row of that table. The fixed-layout model uses the following simple steps:

1. Any column element whose `width` property has a value other than `auto` sets the width for that column.
2. If a column has an `auto` width, but the cell in the first row of the table within that column has a `width` other than `auto`, then that cell sets the width for that column. If the cell spans multiple columns, then the width is divided equally among the columns.
3. Any columns that are still auto-sized are sized so that their widths are as equal as possible.

At that point, the width of the table is set to be either the value of `width` for the table or the sum of the column widths, whichever is greater. If the table turns out to be wider than the column widths, the difference is divided by the number of columns and added to each of them.

Automatic Table Layout

The automatic-layout model, while not as fast as fixed-layout, is likely to be much more familiar to authors, because it's substantially the same model that HTML tables have used for years. In most current user agents, use of this model will be triggered by a table with a `width` of `auto`, regardless of the value of `table-layout`—although this is not assured.

The details of the model can be expressed in the following steps:

1. For each cell in a column, calculate both the minimum and maximum cell width.
2. Determine the minimum width required to display the content. In determining this minimum content width,

the content can flow to any number of lines, but it may not stick out of the cell's box. If the cell has a `width` value that is larger than the minimum possible width, then the minimum cell width is set to the value of `width`. If the cell's `width` value is `auto`, then the minimum cell width is set to the minimum content width.

3. For the maximum width, determine the width required to display the content without any line-breaking, other than that forced by explicit line-breaking (e.g., due to the `<br>` element). That value is the maximum cell width.

4. For each column, calculate both the minimum and maximum column width.

   a. The column's minimum width is determined by the largest minimum cell width of the cells within the column. If the column has been given an explicit `width` value that is larger than any of the minimum cell widths within the column, then the minimum column width is set to the value of `width`.

   b. For the maximum width, take the largest maximum cell width of the cells within the column. If the column has been given an explicit `width` value that is larger than any of the maximum cell widths within the column, then the maximum column width is set to the value of `width`. These two behaviors recreate the traditional HTML table behavior of forcibly expanding any column to be as wide as its widest cell.

5. In cases where a cell spans more than one column, the sum of the minimum column widths must be equal to the minimum cell width for the spanning cell. Similarly, the sum of the maximum column widths must equal the spanning cell's maximum width. User agents should divide any changes in column widths equally among the spanned columns.

In addition, the user agent must take into account that when a column width has a percentage value for its `width`, the percentage is calculated in relation to the width of the table—even though that width is not yet known. The user agent must hang on to the percentage value and use it in the next part of the algorithm. Once the user agent has determined how wide or narrow each column can be, it can then calculate the width of the table. This happens as follows:

1. If the computed width of the table is not `auto`, then the computed table width is compared to the sum of all the column widths plus any borders and cell-spacing. (Columns with percentage widths are likely calculated at this time.) The larger of the two values is the final width of the table. If the table's computed width is larger than the sum of the column widths, borders, and cell-spacing, then all columns are increased in width by an equal amount so they fill the computed width of the table.
2. If the computed width of the table is `auto`, then the final width of the table is determined by summing up the column widths, borders, and cell-spacing. This means the table will be only as wide as needed to display its content, just as with traditional HTML tables. Any columns with percentage widths use that percentage as a constraint, but it is a constraint that a user agent does not have to satisfy.

Once the last step is completed, then (and only then) can the user agent actually lay out the table.

Collapsing Cell Borders

The collapsing cell model largely describes how HTML tables have always been laid out when they have no cell-spacing. The rules that govern this model are:

- Table elements cannot have any padding, although they can have margins. Thus, there is never separation between the border around the outside of the table and its outermost cells.

- Borders can be applied to cells, rows, row groups, columns, and column groups. The `table` element itself can, as always, have a border.
- There is never any separation between cell borders. In fact, borders collapse into each other where they adjoin, so that only one of the collapsing borders is actually drawn. This is somewhat akin to margin-collapsing, where the largest margin wins. When cell borders collapse, the "most interesting" border wins.
- Once they are collapsed, the borders between cells are centered on the hypothetical grid lines between the cells.

Collapsing borders

When two or more borders are adjacent, they collapse into each other, as shown in Figure 5. There are some strict rules governing which borders will win, and which will not.

1. If one of the collapsing borders has a `border-style` of `hidden`, it takes precedence over all other collapsing borders: all borders at this location are hidden.
2. If one of the collapsing borders has a `border-style` of `none`, it takes the lowest priority. There will be no border drawn at this location only if the all of the borders meeting at this location have a value of `none`. Note that `none` is the default value for `border-style`.
3. If at least one of the collapsing borders has a value other than either `none` or `hidden`, then narrow borders lose out to wider ones. If two or more of the collapsing borders have the same width, then the border style is taken in the following order, from most- to least-preferred: `double`, `solid`, `dashed`, `dotted`, `ridge`, `outset`, `groove`, `inset`. Thus, if two borders with the same width collapse and one is `dashed` while the other is `outset`, the border at that location will be dashed.

4. If collapsing borders have the same style and width but differ in color, the color used is taken from an element in the following list, from most preferred to least: cell, row, row group, column, column group, table. Thus, if the borders of a cell and a column, identical in every way except color, collapse, then the cell's border color (and style and width) will be used. If the collapsing borders come from the same type of element—such as two row borders with the same style and width, but different colors—then the behavior is not defined; it is left up to each user agent to decide what to do in such cases.

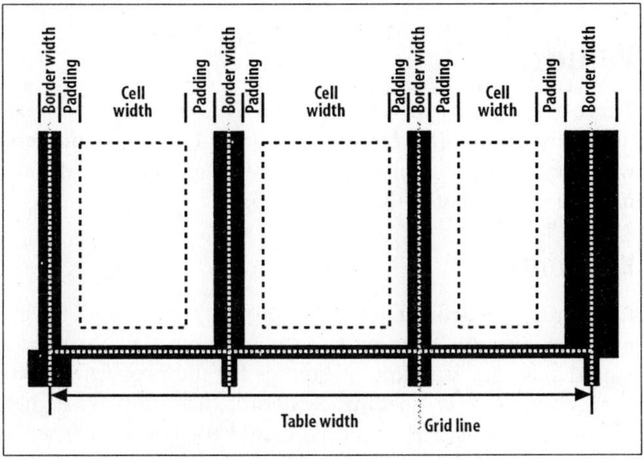

Figure 5. Collapsing cell borders model

Vertical Alignment Within Cells

The following describes the detailed process for aligning cell contents within a row:

1. If any of the cells are baseline-aligned, then the row's baseline is determined and the content of the baseline-aligned cells is placed.

2. Any top-aligned cell has its content placed. The row now has a provisional height, which is defined by the lowest cell bottom of the cells that have already had their content placed.
3. If any remaining cells are middle- or bottom-aligned, and the content height is taller than the provisional row height, the height of the row is increased to enclose the tallest of those cells.
4. All remaining cells have their content placed. In any cell with contents shorter than the row height, the cell's padding is increased in order to match the height of the row.

Values

There are a variety of value types in CSS, most of which use units. By combining basic value types (such as numbers) with units (such as pixels), it becomes possible to do any number of interesting things with CSS.

Keywords

Keywords are defined on a per-property basis and have a meaning specific only to a given property. For example, `normal` has totally unique meanings for the properties `font-variant` and `letter-spacing`. Keywords, like property names, are not case-sensitive. A special case is the keyword `inherit`, which is allowed on all properties and always has the same meaning (get the `property` value from the element's parent).

Color Values

#RRGGBB

This is a hex-pair notation familiar to authors using traditional HTML. In this format, the first pair of digits corresponds to the red setting, the second pair to green, and the third pair to blue. Each pair is in hexadecimal notation in the range 00 – FF. Thus, a "pure" blue would be written #0000FF, "pure" red is written #FF0000, and so on.

#RGB
: This is a shorter form of the six-digit notation described above. In this format, each digit is replicated to arrive at an equivalent six-digit value; thus, #F8C becomes #FF88CC.

rgb(rrr.rr%,ggg.gg%,bbb.bb%)
: This format allows the author to use RGB values in the range 0% to 100%, with decimal values allowed (e.g., 75.5%). The value for black would thus be rgb(0%,0%,0%), whereas "pure" blue would be rgb(0%,0%,100%).

rgb(rrr,ggg,bbb)
: Similar to the previous value, the difference here is that the accepted range of values is 0–255. Not coincidentally, this range is the decimal equivalent of 00–FF in hexadecimal. In this format, "pure" green would be rgb(0,255,0), and white would be represented as rgb(255,255,255).

<keyword>
: One of 17 recognized keywords based largely on the original Windows VGA colors. These keywords are: aqua, black, blue, fuchsia, gray, green, lime, maroon, navy, olive, orange, purple, red, silver, teal, white, and yellow. Browsers may recognize other keywords, such as the X11 color keywords that are documented in the W3C CSS3 Color module specification.

Number Values

A number value is expressed as a positive or negative number (when permitted). Numbers can be either real or integers, and some properties may restrict number values to integers. They may also restrict the range of acceptable values, as with color values that accept only integers in the range 0–255.

Percentage Values

A percentage value is expressed as a positive or negative number (when permitted), followed immediately by a percent sign (`%`). There should never be any space between the number and the percent sign. A percentage value will always be computed relative to something else. For example, declaring `font-size: 120%;` for an element sets the font size of that element at 120% the `font-size` of its parent element.

Length Values

A length value is expressed as a positive or negative number (when permitted), followed immediately by a two-letter abbreviation that represents the units to be used. There should never be any space between the number and the unit designator. Note that a value of `0` (zero) need not have a unit designator. Length units are divided into two types: *absolute units*, which are always measured in the same way, and *relative units*, which are measured in relation to other things.

Absolute length units

Inches (`in`*)*
: As you might expect, the same inches found on typical U.S. rulers. The mapping from inches to a monitor or other display device is usually approximate at best, since many systems have no concept of the relation of their display areas to "real-world" measurements such as inches. Thus, inches should be used with extreme caution in screen design.

Centimeters (`cm`*)*
: The centimeters found on rulers the world over. There are 2.54 cm to an inch, and one centimeter equals 0.394 inches. The same mapping warnings that applied to inches also apply to centimeters.

Millimeters (mm)
: There are 10 millimeters to a centimeter, so you get 25.4 mm to an inch, and 1 millimeter equals 0.0394 inches. Bear in mind the previous warnings about mapping lengths to monitors.

Points (pt)
: Points are standard typographical measures used by printers and typesetters for decades and by word-processing programs for many years. By modern definition, there are 72 points to an inch. Therefore, the capital letters of text set to 12 points should be a sixth of an inch tall. For example, `P {font-size: 18pt;}` is equivalent to `P {font-size: 0.25in;}`, assuming proper mapping of lengths to the display environment (see comments above).

Picas (pc)
: Another typographical term. A pica is equivalent to 12 points, which means there are 6 picas to an inch. The capital letters of text set to 1 pica should be a sixth of an inch tall. For example, `P {font-size: 1.5pc;}` would set text to be the same size as the example declarations found in the definition of points. Keep in mind previous warnings.

Relative length units

em-height (em)
: This refers to the em-height of a given font. In CSS, the em-height is equivalent to the height of the character box for a given font. Ems can be used to set relative sizes for fonts; for example, `1.2em` is the same as saying `120%`.

x-height (ex)
: This refers to the x-height of the font. However, the vast majority of fonts do not include their x-height, so many browsers approximate it (poorly) by simply setting `1ex` to be equal to `0.5em`. The exception is IE5/Mac, which

attempts to determine the actual x-height of a font by bit-mapping an "x" and counting pixels!

Pixels (px)
: A pixel is a small box on screen, but CSS defines pixels more abstractly. In CSS terms, a pixel is defined to be about the size required to yield 96 pixels per inch. Most user agents ignore this definition in favor of simply addressing the pixels on the monitor. Scaling factors are brought into play when printing, although this scale cannot be relied upon.

URLs

url (<url>)
: Used to point to a file such as a graphic. CSS defines URLs as relative to the stylesheet, but Netscape Navigator 4.x interprets URLs relative to the document being styled. Thanks to this bug, it is often recommended that absolute URLs be used instead of relative URLs.

Aural-Specific Values

The following values are used in conjunction with aural style properties in CSS2. These values were dropped from CSS2.1 due to a lack of support and are included here for the sake of completeness.

Angle values
: Used to define the position from which a given sound should seem to originate. There are three type of angles: degrees (`deg`), grads (`grad`), and radians (`rad`). For example, a right angle could be declared as `90deg`, `100grad`, or `1.57rad`; in each case, the values are translated into degrees in the range 0 through 360. This is also true of negative values, which are allowed. The measure `-90deg` is the same as `270deg`.

Time values
: Used to specify delays between speaking elements; can be expressed as either milliseconds (ms) or seconds (s). Thus, 100ms and 0.1s are equivalent. Time values may not be negative, as CSS is supposed to avoid paradoxes.

Frequency values
: Used to declare frequencies for the sounds that speaking browsers can produce. Frequency values can be expressed as hertz (Hz) or megahertz (mHz) and cannot be negative. The value labels are case-insensitive, so 10mHz and 10mhz are equivalent.

Selectors

Universal Selector

Pattern:

*

Description:

This selector matches any element name in the document's language. If a rule does not have an explicit selector, then the universal selector is inferred.

Examples:

```
* {color: red;}
div * p {color: blue;}
```

Type Selector

Pattern:

element1

Description:

This selector matches the name of an element in the document's language. Every instance of the element name is matched. (CSS1 referred to these as "element selectors.")

Examples:

```
body {background: #FFF;}
p {font-size: 1em;}
```

Descendant Selector

Pattern:

```
element1 element2
```

Description:

This allows the author to select an element based on its status as a descendant of another element. The matched element can be a child, grandchild, great-grandchild, etc., of the ancestor element. (CSS1 referred to these as "contextual selectors.")

Examples:

```
body h1 {font-size: 200%;}
table tr td div ul li {color: purple;}
```

Child Selector

Pattern:

```
element1 > element2
```

Description:

This type of selector is used to match an element based on its status as a child of another element. This is more restrictive than a descendant selector, since only a child will be matched.

Examples:

```
div > p {color: cyan;}
ul > li {font-weight: bold;}
```

Adjacent Sibling Selector

Pattern:

```
element1 + element2
```

Description:

This allows the author to select an element that is the following adjacent sibling of another element. Any text between the two elements is ignored; only elements and their positions in the document tree are considered.

Examples:

```
table + p {margin-top: 2.5em;}
h1 + * {margin-top: 0;}
```

Class Selector

Pattern:

```
element1.classname
element1.classname1.classname2
```

Description:

In languages that permit it, such as HTML, XHTML, SVG, and MathML, a class selector using "dot notation" can be used to select elements that have a class containing a specific value or values. The name of the class value must immediately follow the dot. Multiple class values can be chained together. If no element name precedes the dot, then the selector matches all elements containing that class value or values.

Examples:

```
p.urgent {color: red;}
a.external {font-style: italic;}
.example {background: olive;}
.note.caution {background: yellow;}
```

ID Selector

Pattern:

`element1#idname`

Description:

In languages that permit it, such as HTML or XHTML, an ID selector using "hash notation" can be used to select elements that have an ID containing a specific value or values. The name of the ID value must immediately follow the octothorpe (#). If no element name precedes the octothorpe, then the selector matches all elements containing that ID value.

Examples:

```
h1#page-title {font-size: 250%;}
body#home {background: silver;}
#example {background: lime;}
```

Simple Attribute Selector

Pattern:

`element1[attr]`

Description:

This allows authors to select any element based on the presence of an attribute, regardless of the attribute's value.

Examples:

```
a[rel] {border-bottom: 3px double gray;}
p[class] {border: 1px dotted silver;}
```

Exact Attribute Value Selector

Pattern:

`element1[attr="value"]`

Description:

This allows authors to select any element based on the precise and complete value of an attribute.

Examples:

```
a[rel="Start"] {font-weight: bold;}
p[class="urgent"] {color: red;}
```

Partial Attribute Value Selector

Pattern:

`element1[attr~="value"]`

Description:

This allows authors to select any element based on a portion of the space-separated value of an attribute. Note that `[class~="value"]` is equivalent to `.value` (see above).

Examples:

```
a[rel~="friend"] {text-transform: uppercase;}
p[class~="warning"] {background: yellow;}
```

Language Attribute Selector

Pattern:

`element1[lang|="lc"]`

Description:

This allows authors to select any element with a `lang` attribute whose value is a hyphen-separated list of values, starting with the value provided in the selector.

Examples:

```
html[lang|="tr"] {color: red;}
```

Pseudo-Classes and Pseudo-Elements

:active

Type: Pseudo-class.

Applies to:

An element that is being activated.

Description:

This applies to an element during the period in which it is being activated. The most common example is clicking on a hyperlink in an HTML document: while the mouse button is being held down, the link is active. There are other ways to activate elements, and other elements can in theory be activated, although CSS doesn't define these.

Examples:

```
a:active {color: red;}
*:active {background: blue;}
```

:after

Type: Pseudo-element.

Generates:

A pseudo-element containing generated content placed after the content in the element.

Description:

This allows the author to insert generated content at the end of an element's content. By default, the pseudo-element is inline, but this can be changed using the property `display`.

Examples:

```
a.external:after {content: " " url(/icons/globe.gif);)
p:after {content: " | ";}
```

:before

Type: Pseudo-element.

Generates:

A pseudo-element containing generated content placed before the content in the element.

Description:

This allows the author to insert generated content at the beginning of an element's content. By default, the pseudo-element is inline, but this can be changed using the property `display`.

Examples:

```
a[href]:before {content: "[LINK] ";)
p:before {content: attr(class);}
a[rel~="met"]:after {content: " *";}
```

:first-child

Type: Pseudo-class.

Applies to:

Any element that is the first child of another element.

Description:

With this pseudo-class, an element is matched only when it is the first child of another element. For example, `p:first-child` will select any `p` element that is the first child of some other element. It does *not*, as is commonly assumed, select whatever element is the first child of a paragraph; for that, an author would write `p > *:first-child`.

Examples:

```
body *:first-child {font-weight: bold;}
p:first-child {font-size: 125%;}
```

:first-letter

Type: Pseudo-element.

Generates:

A pseudo-element that contains the first letter of an element.

Description:

This is used to style the first letter of an element. Any leading punctuation should be styled along with the first letter. Some languages have letter combinations that should be treated as a single character, and a user agent may apply the first letter style to both. Prior to CSS2.1, `:first-letter` could be attached only to block-level elements. CSS2.1 expands its scope to include block, list-item, table-call, table caption, and inline-block elements. There is a limited set of properties that can apply to a first letter.

Examples:

```
h1:first-letter {font-size: 166%;}
p:first-letter {text-decoration: underline;}
```

:first-line

Type: Pseudo-element.

Generates:

A pseudo-element that contains the first formatted line of an element.

Description:

This is used to style the first line of text in an element, no matter how many or few words may appear in that line. `:first-line` can be attached only to block-level elements. There is a limited set of properties that can apply to a first line.

Examples:

```
p.lead:first-line {font-weight: bold;}
```

:focus

Type: Pseudo-class.

Applies to: An element that has focus.

Description:

This applies to an element during the period in which it has focus. One example from HTML is an input box that has the text-input cursor within it such that when the user starts typing, text will be entered into that box. Other elements, such as hyperlinks, can also have focus; however, CSS does not define which elements may have focus.

Examples:

```
a:focus {outline: 1px dotted red;}
input:focus {background: yellow;}
```

:hover

Type: Pseudo-class.

Applies to: An element that is in a hovered state.

Description:

This applies to an element during the period in which it is being *hovered* (when the user is designating an element without activating it). The most common example of this is moving the mouse pointer inside the boundaries of a hyperlink in an HTML document. Other elements can in theory be hovered, although CSS doesn't define which ones.

Examples:

```
a[href]:hover {text-decoration: underline;}
p:hover {background: yellow;}
```

:lang

Type: Pseudo-class.

Applies to: Any element with associated language-encoding information.

Description:

This matches elements based on their human-language encoding. Such language information must be contained within or otherwise associated with the document; it cannot be assigned from CSS. The handling of `:lang` is the same as for |= attribute selectors. For example, in an HTML document the language of an element is determined by its `lang` attribute. If the document does not have one, the language of an element is determined by the `lang` attribute of its nearest ancestor that does have one, and lacking that, by the `Content-Language` HTTP header response field (or the respective `meta http-equiv`) for the document.

Examples:

```
html:lang(en) {background: silver;}
*:lang(fr) {quotes: '« ' ' »';}
```

:link

Type: Pseudo-class.

Applies to: A hyperlink to another resource that has not been visited.

Description:

This applies to a link to a URI that has not been visited; that is, the URI to which the link points does not appear in the user agent's history. This state is mutually exclusive with the `:visited` state.

Examples:

```
a:link {color: blue;}
*:link {text-decoration: underline;}
```

:visited

Type: Pseudo-class.

Applies to: A hyperlink to another resource that has already been visited.

Description:

This applies to a link to a URI that has been visited; that is, the URI to which the link points appears in the user agent's history. This state is mutually exclusive with the `:link` state.

Examples:

```
a:visited {color: purple;}
*:visited {color: gray;}
```

Property Reference

Visual Media

background

Values:

[<background-color> || <background-image> || <background-repeat> || <background-attachment> || <background-position>] | `inherit`

Initial value: Refer to individual properties.

Applies to: All elements.

Inherited: No.

Percentages:

Values are allowed for <background-position>.

Computed value: See individual properties.

Description:

A shorthand way of expressing the various background properties using a single rule. Use of this property is encouraged over the other background properties because it is more widely supported and doesn't take as long to type. However, using it will set all of the allowed values (e.g., the repeat, position, and so on) to their defaults if the values are not explicitly declared. Thus the following two rules will have the same appearance:

```
background: yellow;
background: yellow none top left repeat;
```

Furthermore, these defaults can override previous declarations made with more specific background properties. For example, given the following rules:

```
H1 {background-repeat: repeat-x;}
H1, H2 {background: yellow url(headback.gif);}
```

the repeat value for both `h1` and `h2` elements will be set to the default of `repeat`, overriding the previously declared value of `repeat-x`.

Navigator 4.x is infamous for its inability to correctly render backgrounds. If there is no border around an element, then the background will only be visible behind the text of the element, instead of throughout the entire content area and padding. Unfortunately, if a border is added, there will be a transparent gap between the content area and the border itself. This is not the padding, and there is no way to get rid of the gap.

Examples:

```
BODY {background: white url(bg41.gif) fixed center repeat-
x;}
P {background: url(http://www.pix.org/stone.png) #555;}
PRE {background: yellow;}
```

background-attachment

Values:

`scroll` | `fixed` | `inherit`

Initial value: `scroll`

Applies to: All elements.

Inherited: No.

Computed value: As specified.

Description:

This property defines whether the background image scrolls along with the element when the document is scrolled. This property can be used to create "aligned" backgrounds; see *Chapter 9* of *Cascading Style Sheets: The Definitive Guide*, Second Edition (O'Reilly), for more details.

Examples:

```
body {background-attachment: scroll;}
div.fixbg {background-attachment: fixed;}
```

background-color

Values:

<color> | `transparent` | `inherit`

Initial value: `transparent`

Applies to: All elements.

Inherited: No.

Computed value: As specified.

Description:

This property sets a solid color for the background of the element. This color fills the content, padding, and border areas of the element, extending to the outer edge of the element's border. Borders that have transparent sections (such as dashed borders) will show the background color through the transparent sections.

Navigator 4.x insists on applying this value to the parent of an element, not the element itself. This can lead to "holes" in the parent element's background. Opera 4 has a bug that only shows up when a background has been repeated, and the rest of the background of the element is transparent (either by default or when explicitly declared). Scrolling the element "offscreen" and then bringing it back can cause "holes" to be punched through the repeated images of ancestor elements, thus creating visual anomalies.

Examples:

```
h4 {background-color: white;}
p {background-color: rgb(50%,50%,50%);}
pre {background-color: #FF9;}
```

background-image

Values:

<uri> | none | inherit

Initial value: none

Applies to: All elements.

Inherited: No.

Computed value: Absolute URI.

Description:

Places an image in the background of the element. Depending on the value of background-repeat, the image may tile infinitely, along one axis, or not at all. The initial background image (the origin image) is placed according to the value of background-position.

Examples:

```
body {background-image: url(bg41.gif);}
h2 {background-image: url(http://www.pix.org/dots.png);}
```

background-position

Values:

[[<percentage> | <length> | left | center | right] [<percentage> | <length> | top | center | bottom]?] | [[left | center | right] || [top | center | bottom]] | inherit

Initial value: 0%0%

Applies to: Block-level and replaced elements.

Inherited: No.

Percentages:

Refer to the corresponding point on both the element and the origin image.

Computed value:

The absolute length offsets if <length> is specified; otherwise, percentage values.

Description:

This property sets the position of the background's origin image (as defined by `background-image`); this is the point from which any background repetition or tiling will occur. Percentage values define not only a point within the element, but also the same point in the origin image itself, thus allowing (for example) an image to be centered by declaring its position to be `50% 50%`. See Chapter 9 of *Cascading Style Sheets: The Definitive Guide*, Second Edition (O'Reilly), for more details.

When percentage or length values are used, the first is always the horizontal position, and the second the vertical. If only one value is given, it sets the horizontal position, while the missing value is assumed to be either `center` or `50%`. Negative values are permitted, and may place the origin image outside the element's content area without actually rendering it.

Examples:

```
body {background-position: top center;}
div#navbar {background-position: right;}
pre {background-position: 10px 50%;}
```

background-repeat

Values:

`repeat` | `repeat-x` | `repeat-y` | `no-repeat` | `inherit`

Initial value: `no-repeat`

Applies to: All elements.

Inherited: No.

Computed value: As specified.

Description:

This property defines the tiling pattern for the background image. Note that the axis-related repeat values actually cause repetition in both directions along the relevant axis. The repetition begins from the origin image, which is defined as the value of `background-image` and is placed according to the value of `background-position`.

Examples:

```
body {background-repeat: no-repeat;}
h2 {background-repeat: repeat-x;}
ul {background-repeat: repeat-y;}
```

border

Values:

[<border-width> || <border-style> || <border-color>] | `inherit`

Initial value: Refer to individual properties.

Applies to: All elements.

Inherited: No.

Computed value: As specified.

Description:

This is a shorthand property that defines the width, color, and style of an element's border. Note that while none of the values are actually required, omitting a border style will result in no border being applied because the default border style is `none`. IE4 and IE5.0/Win do not apply borders to inline elements; IE5/Mac and IE5.5+/Win do apply borders to inline elements.

Examples:

```
h1 {border: 2px dashed olive;}
a:link {border: blue solid 1px;}
p.warning {border: double 5px red;}
```

border-bottom

Values:

[<border-width> || <border-style> || <border-color>] | `inherit`

Initial value: Not defined for shorthand properties.

Applies to: All elements.

Inherited: No.

Computed value:

See individual properties (`border-width`, etc.).

Description:

This shorthand property defines the width, color, and style of the bottom border of an element. As with `border`, omission of a border style will result in no border appearing.

Examples:

```
ul {border-bottom: 0.5in groove green;}
a:active {border-bottom: purple 2px dashed;}
```

border-bottom-color

Values:

<color> | `transparent` | `inherit`

Initial value: The value of `color` for the element.

Applies to: All elements.

Inherited: No.

Computed value:

If no value is specified, use the computed value of the property `color` for the same element; otherwise, as specified.

Description:

This property sets the color for the visible portions of the bottom border of an element. Only a solid color can be defined, and the border's style must be something other than none or hidden for any visible border to appear.

Examples:

```
ul {border-bottom-color: green;}
a:active {border-bottom-color: purple;}
```

---

border-bottom-style

Values:

none | hidden | dotted | dashed | solid | double | groove | ridge | inset | outset | inherit

Initial value: none

Applies to: All elements.

Inherited: No.

Computed value: As specified.

Description:

This defines the style for the bottom border of an element. The value must be something other than none for any border to appear. In CSS1, HTML user agents were required to support only solid and none.

Examples:

```
ul {border-bottom-style: groove;}
a:active {border-bottom-style: dashed;}
```

---

border-bottom-width

Values:

thin | medium | thick | <length> | inherit

Initial value: medium

Applies to: All elements.

Inherited: No.

Computed value:

Absolute length; 0 if the style of the border is none or hidden.

Description:

This property sets the width for the bottom border of an element, which will take effect only if the border's style is something other than none. If the border style is none, then the border width is effectively reset to 0. Negative length values are not permitted.

Examples:

```
ul {border-bottom-width: 0.5in;}
a:active {border-bottom-width: 2px;}
```

border-color

Values:

[<color> | transparent]{1,4} | inherit

Initial value: Not defined for shorthand properties.

Applies to: All elements.

Inherited: No.

Computed value:

See individual properties (border-top-color, etc.).

Description:

This shorthand property sets the color for the visible portions of the overall border of an element or sets a different color for each of the four sides. Remember that a border's style must be something other than none or hidden for any visible border to appear.

Examples:

```
h1 {border-color: purple;}
a:visited {border-color: maroon;}
```

border-left

Values:

[<border-width> || <border-style> || <border-color>] | `inherit`

Initial value: Not defined for shorthand properties.

Applies to: All elements.

Inherited: No.

Computed value: See individual properties (`border-width`, etc.).

Description:

This shorthand property defines the width, color, and style of the left border of an element. As with `border`, omission of a border style will result in no border appearing.

Examples:

```
p {border-left: 3em solid gray;}
pre {border-left: double black 4px;}
```

border-left-color

Values:

<color> | `transparent` | `inherit`

Initial value: The value of `color` for the element.

Applies to: All elements.

Inherited: No.

Computed value:

If no value is specified, use the computed value of the property `color` for the same element; otherwise, as specified.

Description:

This property sets the color for the visible portions of the left border of an element. Only a solid color can be defined, and the border's style must be something other than none or hidden for any visible border to appear.

Examples:

```
p {border-left-color: gray;}
pre {border-left-color: black;}
```

border-left-style

Values:

none | hidden | dotted | dashed | solid | double | groove | ridge | inset | outset | inherit

Initial value: none

Applies to: All elements.

Inherited: No.

Computed value: As specified.

Description:

This defines the style for the left border of an element. The value must be something other than none for any border to appear. In CSS1, HTML user agents were required to support only solid and none.

Examples:

```
p {border-left-style: solid;}
pre {border-left-style: double;}
```

border-left-width

Values:

thin | medium | thick | <length> | inherit

Initial value: medium

Applies to: All elements.

Inherited: No.

Computed value:

Absolute length; 0 if the style of the border is none or hidden.

Description:

This sets the width for the left border of an element, which will take effect only if the border's style is something other than none. If the border style is none, then the border width is effectively reset to 0. Negative length values are not permitted.

Examples:

```
p {border-left-width: 3em;}
pre {border-left-width: 4px;}
```

border-right

Values:

[<border-width> || <border-style> || <border-color>] | inherit

Initial value: Not defined for shorthand properties.

Applies to: All elements.

Inherited: No.

Computed value: See individual properties (border-width, etc.).

Description:

This shorthand property defines the width, color, and style of the right border of an element. As with border, omission of a border style will result in no border appearing.

Examples:

```
img {border-right: 30px dotted blue;}
h3 {border-right: cyan 1em inset;}
```

border-right-color

Values:

<color> | transparent | inherit

Initial value: The value of color for the element.

Applies to: All elements.

Inherited: No.

Computed value:

If no value is specified, use the computed value of the property color for the same element; otherwise, as specified.

Description:

This property sets the color for the visible portions of the right border of an element. Only a solid color can be defined, and the border's style must be something other than none or hidden for any visible border to appear.

Examples:

```
img {border-right-color: blue;}
h3 {border-right-color: cyan;}
```

border-right-style

Values:

none | hidden | dotted | dashed | solid | double | groove | ridge | inset | outset | inherit

Initial value: none

Applies to: All elements.

Inherited: No.

Computed value: As specified.

Description:

This defines the style for the right border of an element. The value must be something other than none for any border to appear. In CSS1, HTML user agents were required to support only solid and none.

Examples:

```
img {border-right-style: dotted;}
h3 {border-right-style: inset;}
```

border-right-width

Values:

thin | medium | thick | <length> | inherit

Initial value: medium

Applies to: All elements.

Inherited: No.

Computed value:

Absolute length; 0 if the style of the border is none or hidden.

Description:

This sets the width for the right border of an element, which will take effect only if the border's style is something other than none. If the border style is none, then the border width is effectively reset to 0. Negative length values are not permitted.

Examples:

```
img {border-right-width: 30px;}
h3 {border-right-width: 1em;}
```

border-style

Values:

[none | hidden | dotted | dashed | solid | double | groove | ridge | inset | outset]{1,4} | inherit

Initial value: Not defined for shorthand properties.

Applies to: All elements.

Inherited: No.

Computed value:

See individual properties (`border-top-style`, etc.).

Description:

This shorthand property can be used to set the styles for the overall border of an element or for each side individually. The value of any border must be something other than `none` for the border to appear.

Note that setting `border-style` to `none` (its default value) will result in no border at all. In such a case, any value of `border-width` will be ignored and the width of the border set to `0`. CCS1 requires HTML users agents to support only `solid` and `none`. Any unrecognized value from the list of values should be reinterpreted as `solid`.

Navigator 4.x does not reset the `border-width` to `0` if `border-style` is `none`, but instead incorrectly honors the width setting.

Examples:

```
h1 {border-style: solid;}
img {border-style: inset;}
```

border-top

Values:

[<border-width> || <border-style> || <border-color>] | `inherit`

Initial value: Not defined for shorthand properties.

Applies to: All elements.

Inherited: No.

Computed value: See individual properties (`border-width`, etc.).

Description:

This shorthand property defines the width, color, and style of the top border of an element. As with `border`, omission of a border style will result in no border appearing.

Examples:

```
ul {border-top: 0.5in solid black;}
h1 {border-top: dashed 1px gray;}
```

border-top-color

Values:

<color> | `transparent` | `inherit`

Initial value: The value of `color` for the element.

Applies to: All elements.

Inherited: No.

Computed value:

If no value is specified, use the computed value of the property `color` for the same element; otherwise, as specified.

Description:

This property sets the color for the visible portions of the top border of an element. Only a solid color can be defined, and the border's style must be something other than `none` or `hidden` for any visible border to appear.

Examples:

```
ul {border-top-color: black;}
h1 {border-top-color: gray;}
```

border-top-style

Values:

`none` | `hidden` | `dotted` | `dashed` | `solid` | `double` | `groove` | `ridge` | `inset` | `outset` | `inherit`

Initial value: `none`

Applies to: All elements.

Inherited: No.

Computed value: As specified.

Description:

This defines the style for the top border of an element. The value must be something other than `none` for any border to appear. In CSS1, HTML user agents were required to support only `solid` and `none`.

Examples:

```
ul {border-top-style: solid;}
h1 {border-top-style: dashed;}
```

border-top-width

Values:

`thin` | `medium` | `thick` | <length> | `inherit`

Initial value: `medium`

Applies to: All elements.

Inherited: No.

Computed value:

Absolute length; `0` if the style of the border is `none` or `hidden`.

Description:

This sets the width for the top border of an element, which will take effect only if the border's style is something other than `none`. If the style is `none`, then the width is effectively reset to `0`. Negative length values are not permitted.

Examples:

```
ul {border-top-width: 0.5in;}
h1 {border-top-width: 1px;}
```

border-width

Values:

[thin | medium | thick | <length>]{1,4} | inherit

Initial value: Not defined for shorthand properties.

Applies to: All elements.

Inherited: No.

Computed value:

See individual properties (border-top-style, etc.).

Description:

This shorthand property can be used to set the width for the overall border of an element or for each side individually. The width will take effect for a given border only if the border's style is something other than none. If the border style is none, then the border width is effectively reset to 0. Negative length values are not permitted.

Examples:

```
h1 {border-width: 2ex;}
img {border-width: 5px;}
```

bottom

Values:

<length> | <percentage> | auto | inherit

Initial value: auto

Applies to:

Positioned elements (that is, elements for which the value of position is something other than static).

Inherited: No.

Percentages: Refer to the height of the containing block.

Computed value:

For relatively positioned elements, see note; for `static` elements, `auto`; for length values, the corresponding absolute length; for percentage values, the specified value; otherwise, `auto`.

Note:

For relatively positioned elements, if both `bottom` and `top` are `auto`, their computed values are both `0`; if one of them is `auto`, it becomes the negative of the other; if neither is `auto`, `bottom` will become the negative of the value of `top`.

Description:

This property defines the offset between the bottom outer margin edge of a positioned element and the bottom edge of its containing block.

Examples:

```
div#footer {position: fixed; bottom: 0;}
sup {position: relative; bottom: 0.5em; vertical-align:
baseline;}
```

clear

Values:

`left` | `right` | `both` | `none`

Initial value: `none`

Applies to: Block-level elements.

Inherited: No.

Computed value: As specified.

Description:

This defines the sides of an element on which no floating elements may appear. In CSS1 and CSS2, this is accomplished by automatically increasing the top margin of the cleared element. In CSS2.1, clearance space is added above the element's top margin, but the margin itself is not altered. In either case, the end result is that the element's top outer border edge is just below the bottom outer margin edge of a floated element on the declared side.

Examples:

```
h1 {clear: both;}
h3 {clear: right;}
```

clip

Values:

`rect(`*`top`*`, `*`right`*`, `*`bottom`*`, `*`left`*`)` | `auto` | `inherit`

Initial value: `auto`

Applies to:

Absolutely positioned elements (in CSS2, `clip` applied to block-level and replaced elements).

Inherited: No.

Computed value:

For a rectangle, a set of four computed lengths representing the edges of the clipping rectangle; otherwise, as specified.

Description:

This is used to define a clipping rectangle inside of which the content of an absolutely positioned element is visible. Content outside this clipping area is treated according to the value of `overflow`. The clipping area can be smaller or larger than the content area of the element.

Examples:

```
div.sidebar {overflow: scroll; clip: 0 0 5em 10em;}
img.tiny {overflow: hidden; clip: 5px 5px 20px 20px;}
```

color

Values:

<color> | `inherit`

Initial value: User agent–specific.

Applies to: All elements.

Inherited: Yes.

Computed value: As specified.

Description:

This property sets the foreground color of an element, which in HTML rendering means the text of an element; raster images are not affected by `color`. This is also the color applied to any borders of the element, unless overridden by `border-color` or one of the other border color properties (`border-top-color`, etc.).

Examples:

```
strong {color: rgb(255,128,128);}
h3 {color: navy;}
p.warning {color: #ff0000;}
pre.pastoral {color: #0f0;}
```

content

Values:

`normal` | [<string> | <uri> | <counter> | `attr(`<identifier>`)`| `open-quote` | `close-quote` | `no-open-quote` | `no-close-quote`]+ | `inherit`

Initial value: `normal`

Applies to: `:before` and `:after` pseudo-elements.

Inherited: No.

Computed value:

For <uri> values, an absolute URI; for attribute references, the resulting string; otherwise, as specified.

Description:

This is the property used to define the generated content placed before or after an element. By default, this is likely to be inline content, but the type of box the content creates can be controlled using the property display.

Examples:

```
p:before {content: "Paragraph...";}
img:after {content: attr(src);}
a[href]:after {content: "(" attr(href) ")"; font-size:
smaller;}
```

counter-increment

Values:

[<identifier> <integer>?]+ | none | inherit

Initial value: User agent–dependent.

Applies to: All elements.

Inherited: No.

Computed value: As specified.

Description:

With this property, counters can be incremented (or decremented) by any value, positive or negative. If no <integer> is supplied, it defaults to 1.

Examples:

```
h1 {counter-increment: section;}
*.backward li {counter-increment: counter -1;}
```

counter-reset

Values:

[<identifier> <integer>?]+ | none | inherit

Initial value: User agent-dependent.

Applies to: All elements.

Inherited: No.

Computed value: As specified.

Description:

With this property, counters can be reset (or set for the first time) to any value, positive or negative. If no <integer> is supplied, it defaults to `0`.

Examples:

```
h1 {counter-reset: section;}
h2 {counter-reset: subsec 1;}
```

---

cursor

Values:

[[<uri>,]* [`auto` | `default` | `pointer` | `crosshair` | `move` | `e-resize` | `ne-resize` | `nw-resize` | `n-resize` | `se-resize` | `sw-resize` | `s-resize` | `w-resize` | `text` | `wait` | `help` | `progress`]] | `inherit`

Initial value: `auto`

Applies to: All elements.

Inherited: Yes.

Computed value:

For <uri> values, an absolute URI; otherwise, as specified.

Description:

This defines the cursor shape to be used when a mouse pointer is placed within the boundary of an element (although CSS2.1 does not define which edge creates this boundary). Authors are cautioned to remember that users are typically very aware of cursor changes, and can be easily confused by changes that seem counterintuitive. For example, making any noninteractive element switch the cursor state to `pointer` is quite likely to cause user frustration.

<uri> values are supported only by IE6/Win as of this writing.

Examples:

```
a.moreinfo {cursor: help;}
a[href].external {cursor: url(globe.ani);}
```

direction

Values:

`ltr | rtl | inherit`

Initial value: `ltr`

Applies to: All elements.

Inherited: Yes.

Computed value: As specified.

Description:

This property specifies the base writing direction of blocks and the direction of embeddings and overrides for the Unicode bidirectional algorithm. User agents that do not support bidirectional text are permitted to ignore this property.

Examples:

```
*:lang(en) {direction: ltr;}
*:lang(ar) {direction: rtl;}
```

display

Values:

`none | inline | block | inline-block | list-item | run-in | table | inline-table | table-row-group | table-header-group | table-footer-group | table-row | table-column-group | table-column | table-cell | table-caption | inherit`

Initial value: `inline`

Applies to: All elements.

Inherited: No.

Computed value:

Varies for floated, positioned, and root elements (see CSS2.1, section 9.7); otherwise, as specified.

Note:

The values `compact` and `marker` appeared in CSS2 but were dropped from CSS2.1 due to a lack of widespread support.

Description:

This is used to define the kind of display box an element generates during layout. Gratuitous use of `display` with a document type such as HTML can be dangerous, as it upsets the display hierarchy already defined in HTML. In the case of XML, which has no such built-in hierarchy, `display` is indispensable.

Examples:

```
h1 {display: block;}
li {display: list-item;}
img {display: inline;}
.hide {display: none;}
tr {table-row;}
```

float

Values:

`left` | `right` | `none` | `inherit`

Initial value: none

Applies to: All elements.

Inherited: No.

Computed value: As specified.

Description:

`float` defines the direction in which an element is floated. This has traditionally been applied to images in order to let text flow around them, but in CSS, any element may be floated. A floated element will generate a block-level box no matter what kind of element it may be. Floated nonreplaced elements should be given an explicit width, as they otherwise tend to become as narrow as possible. Basic floating is generally supported by all browsers, especially on images, but the nature of floats can lead to unexpected results when they are used as a page layout mechanism. Use `float` cautiously and thoroughly test any pages employing it.

Examples:

```
img.figure {float: left;}
p.sidebar {float: right; width: 15em;}
```

---

font

Values:

[[<font-style> || <font-variant> || <font-weight>]? <font-size> [/ <line-height>]? <font-family>] | `caption` | `icon` | `menu` | `message-box` | `small-caption` | `status-bar` | `inherit`

Initial value: Refer to individual properties.

Applies to: All elements.

Inherited: Yes.

Percentages:

Calculated with respect to the parent element for <font-size> and with respect to the element's <font-size> for <line-height>.

Computed value: See individual properties (`font-style`, etc.).

Description:

This is a shorthand property used to set two or more aspects of an element's font all at once. It can also be used to set the element's font to match an aspect of the user's computing environment using keywords such as `icon`. Note that if these keywords are not used, the minimum font value must include the font size and family in that order.

Examples:

```
p {font: small-caps italic bold small/1.25em
Helvetica,sans-serif;}
p.example {font: 14px Arial;} /* technically correct,
although
    generic font-families are encouraged for fallback
purposes */
.figure span {font: icon;}
```

font-family

Values:

[[<family-name> | <generic-family>],]* [<family-name> | <generic-family>] | `inherit`

Initial value: User agent-specific.

Applies to: All elements.

Inherited: Yes.

Computed value: As specified.

Description:

This defines a font family to be used in the display of an element's text. Note that use of a specific font family (e.g., Geneva) is wholly dependent on that family being available on a user's machine; no font downloading is implied by this property. Therefore, the use of generic family names as a fallback is strongly encouraged. Font names that contain spaces or nonalphabetic characters should be quoted in order to minimize potential confusion.

Examples:

```
p {font-family: Helvetica, Arial, sans-serif;}
li {font-family: Times, TimesNR, "New Century Schoolbook",
serif;}
pre {font-family: Courier, "Courier New", "Andale Mono",
Monaco, monospace;}
```

font-size

Values:

`xx-small` | `x-small` | `small` | `medium` | `large` | `x-large` | `xx-large` | `smaller` | `larger` | <length> | <percentage> | `inherit`

Initial value: `medium`

Applies to: All elements.

Inherited: Yes.

Percentages:

Calculated with respect to the parent element's font size.

Computed value: An absolute length.

Description:

This property sets the size of the font. The size can be defined as an absolute size, a relative size, a length value, or a percentage value. Negative length and percentage values are not permitted.

The dangers of font-size assignment are many and varied, and points are particularly discouraged in web design, as there is no certain relationship between points and the pixels on a monitor. Note also that, due to early misunderstandings, setting the `font-size` to `medium` will lead to different results in Internet Explorer and Navigator 4.x. Some of these problems are covered in Chapter 5 of *Cascading Style Sheets: The Definitive Guide*, Second Edition (O'Reilly); for further discussion, refer to *http://style.cleverchimp.com/*.

For best results, authors are encouraged to use either percentages or em units for font sizing. As a last resort, pixel sizes can be used, but this approach has serious accessibility penalties since it prevents users from resizing text in IE/Win, even if it is too small to read comfortably. Most other browsers allow the user to resize text no matter how it has been sized.

Examples:

```
h2 {font-size: 200%;}
code {font-size: 0.9em;}
p.caption {font-size: 9px;}
```

font-style

Values:

`italic | oblique | normal | inherit`

Initial value: `normal`

Applies to: All elements.

Inherited: Yes.

Computed value: As specified.

Description:

This sets the font to use an italic, oblique, or normal font face. Italic text is generally defined as a separate face within the font family. It is theoretically possible for a user agent to compute a slanted font face from the normal face. However, the reality is that user agents rarely recognize the difference between italic and oblique text, and almost always render both in exactly the same way.

Examples:

```
em {font-style: oblique;}
i {font-style: italic;}
```

font-variant

Values:

`small-caps | normal | inherit`

Initial value: `normal`

Applies to: All elements.

Inherited: Yes.

Computed value: As specified.

Description:

This property is basically used to define small-caps text. It is theoretically possible for a user agent to compute a small-caps font face from the normal face.

Examples:

```
h3 {font-variant: small-caps;}
p {font-variant: normal;}
```

font-weight

Values:

`normal` | `bold` | `bolder` | `lighter` | `100` | `200` | `300` | `400` | `500` | `600` | `700` | `800` | `900` | `inherit`

Initial value: `normal`

Applies to: All elements.

Inherited: Yes.

Computed value:

One of the numeric values (`100`, etc.), or one of the numeric values plus one of the relative values (`bolder` or `lighter`).

Description:

This property sets the font weight used in rendering an element's text. The numeric value `400` is equivalent to the keyword `normal`, and `700` is equivalent to `bold`. Each numeric value must be at least as light as the next lowest number and at least as heavy as the next highest number. Thus, if a font has only two weights—normal and bold—then the numbers 100 through 500 will be normal, and 600 through 900 will be bold.

Examples:

```
b {font-weight: 700;}
strong {font-weight: bold;}
.delicate {font-weight: lighter;}
```

height

Values:

<length> | <percentage> | `auto` | `inherit`

Initial value: `auto`

Applies to: Block-level and replaced elements.

Inherited: No.

Percentages: Calculated with respect to the height of the containing block.

Computed value:

For `auto` and percentage values, as specified; otherwise, an absolute length, unless the property does not apply to the element (then `auto`).

Description:

This defines the height of an element's content area, outside of which padding, borders, and margins are added. This property is ignored for inline nonreplaced elements. Negative length and percentage values are not permitted.

Examples:

```
img.icon {height: 50px;}
h1 {height: 1.75em;}
```

left

Values:

<length> | <percentage> | `auto` | `inherit`

Initial value: `auto`

Applies to: Positioned elements (that is, elements for which the value of `position` is something other than `static`).

Inherited: No.

Percentages: Refer to the width of the containing block.

Computed value:

For relatively positioned elements, see note; for `static` elements, `auto`; for length values, the corresponding absolute length; for percentage values, the specified value; otherwise, `auto`.

Note:

For relatively positioned elements, the computed value of `left` always equals -`right`.

Description:

This property defines the offset between the left outer margin edge of a positioned element and the left edge of its containing block.

Examples:

```
div#footer {position: fixed; left: 0;}
*.hanger {position: relative; left: -25px;}
```

letter-spacing

Values:

<length> | `normal` | `inherit`

Initial value: `normal`

Applies to: All elements.

Inherited: Yes.

Computed value: For length values, the absolute length; otherwise, `normal`.

Description:

This defines the amount of whitespace to be inserted between the character boxes of text. Since character glyphs are typically narrower than their character boxes, length values create a modifier to the usual spacing between letters. Thus, `normal` is synonymous with 0. Negative length values are permitted and will cause letters to bunch closer together.

Examples:

```
p.spacious {letter-spacing: 6px;}
em {letter-spacing: 0.2em;}
p.cramped {letter-spacing: -0.5em;}
```

line-height

Values:

<length> | <percentage> | <number> | `normal` | `inherit`

Initial value: `normal`

Applies to: All elements (but see text regarding replaced and block-level elements).

Inherited: Yes.

Percentages: Relative to the font size of the element.

Computed value: For length and percentage values, the absolute value; otherwise, as specified.

Description:

This property influences the layout of line boxes. When applied to a block-level element, it defines the minimum distance between baselines within that element, but not the maximum. The difference between the computed values of `line-height` and `font-size` (called "leading" in CSS) is split in half and added to the top and bottom of each piece of content in a line of text. The shortest box that can enclose all those pieces of content is the line box. A raw number value assigns a scaling factor, which is inherited instead of a computed value. Negative values are not permitted. (Navigator 4.x incorrectly permits negative values for this property.)

Examples:

```
p {line-height: 1.5em;}
h2 {line-height: 200%;}
ul {line-height: 1.2;}
pre {line-height: 0.75em;}
```

list-style

Values:

[<list-style-type> || <list-style-image> || <list-style-position>] | `inherit`

Initial value: Refer to individual properties.

Applies to: Elements whose `display` value is `list-item`.

Inherited: Yes.

Computed value: See individual properties.

Description:

This is a shorthand property that condenses all the other list-style properties. Because it applies to any element that has a `display` of `list-item`, it will apply only to `li` elements in ordinary HTML and XHTML, although it can be applied to any element and inherited by `list-item` elements.

Examples:

```
ul {list-style: square url(bullet3.gif) outer;} /* values
are inherited by 'li' elements */
ol {list-style: upper-roman;}
```

list-style-image

Values:

<uri> | `none` | `inherit`

Initial value: `none`

Applies to: Elements whose `display` value is `list-item`.

Inherited: Yes.

Computed value: For <uri> values, the absolute URI; otherwise, `none`.

Description:

This specifies an image to be used as the marker on an ordered or unordered list item. The placement of the image with respect to the content of the list item can be broadly controlled using `list-style-position`.

Examples:

```
ul {list-style-image: url(bullet3.gif);}
ul li {list-style-image: url(http://example.org/pix/
checkmark.png);}
```

list-style-position

Values:

`inside` | `outside` | `inherit`

Initial value: `outside`

Applies to: Elements whose `display` value is `list-item`.

Inherited: Yes.

Computed value: As specified.

Description:

This property is used to declare the position of the list marker with respect to the content of the list item. Outside markers are placed some distance from the border edge of the list item, but the distance is not defined in CSS. Inside markers are treated as though they were an inline element inserted at the beginning of the list item's content.

Examples:

```
li {list-style-position: outside;}
ol li {list-style-position: inside;}
```

list-style-type

CSS2.1 values:

disc | circle | square | decimal | decimal-leading-zero | lower-roman | upper-roman | lower-greek | lower-latin | armenian | georegian | none | inherit

CSS2 values:

disc | circle | square | decimal | decimal-leading-zero | upper-alpha | lower-alpha | upper-roman | lower-roman | lower-greek| hebrew | armenian | georgian | cjk-ideographic | hiragana | katakana | hiragana-iroha | none | inherit

Initial value: disc

Applies to: Elements whose display value is list-item.

Inherited: Yes.

Computed value: As specified.

Description:

This is used to declare the type of marker system to be used in the presentation of a list. There is no defined behavior for what happens when a list using an alphabetic ordering exceeds the letters in the list. For example, once an upper-latin list reaches "Z", the specification does not say what the next bullet should be. (Two possible answers are "AA" and "ZA".)

Examples:

```
ul {list-style-type: square;}
ol {list-style-type: lower-roman;}
```

margin

Values:

[<length> | <percentage> | auto]{1,4} | inherit

Initial value: Not defined.

Applies to: All elements.

Inherited: No.

Percentages: Refer to the width of the containing block.

Computed value: See individual properties.

Description:

This shorthand property sets the width of the overall margin for an element or sets the widths of each individual side margin. Vertically adjacent margins of block-level elements are collapsed, whereas inline elements effectively do not take top and bottom margins. The left and right margins of inline elements do not collapse, nor do margins on floated elements. Negative margin values are permitted, but caution is warranted, because negative values can cause elements to overwrite other parts of a page or to appear to be wider than their parent elements.

Examples:

```
h1 {margin: 2ex;}
p {margin: auto;}
img {margin: 10px;}
```

---

margin-bottom

Values:

<length> | <percentage> | `auto` | `inherit`

Initial value: `0`

Applies to: All elements.

Inherited: No.

Percentages: Refer to the width of the containing block.

Computed value: For percentages, as specified; for length values, the absolute length.

Description:

This sets the width of the bottom margin for an element. Negative values are permitted, but caution is warranted.

Examples:

```
ul {margin-bottom: 0.5in;}
h1 {margin-bottom: 2%;}
```

margin-left

Values:

<length> | <percentage> | `auto` | `inherit`

Initial value:	`0`
Applies to:	All elements.
Inherited:	No.
Percentages:	Refer to the width of the containing block.
Computed value:	For percentages, as specified; for length values, the absolute length.

Description:

This sets the width of the left margin for an element. Negative values are permitted, but caution is warranted.

Examples:

```
p {margin-left: 5%;}
pre {margin-left: 3em;}
```

margin-right

Values:

<length> | <percentage> | `auto` | `inherit`

Initial value:	`0`
Applies to:	All elements.

Inherited: No.

Percentages: Refer to the width of the containing block.

Computed value: For percentages, as specified; for length values, the absolute length.

Description:

This sets the width of the right margin for an element. Negative values are permitted, but caution is warranted.

Examples:

```
img {margin-right: 30px;}
ol {margin-right: 5em;}
```

margin-top

Values:

<length> | <percentage> | `auto` | `inherit`

Initial value: `0`

Applies to: All elements.

Inherited: No.

Percentages: Refer to the width of the containing block.

Computed value: For percentages, as specified; for length values, the absolute length.

Description:

This sets the width of the top margin for an element. Negative values are permitted, but caution is warranted.

Examples:

```
ul {margin-top: 0.5in;}
h3 {margin-top: 1.5em;}
```

max-height

Values:

<length> | <percentage> | none | inherit

Initial value: none

Applies to: All elements except inline nonreplaced elements and table elements.

Inherited: No.

Percentages: Refer to the height of the containing block.

Computed value: For percentages, as specified; for length values, the absolute length; otherwise, none.

Description:

The value of this property sets a maximum constraint on the height of the element. Thus, the element can be shorter than the specified value, but not taller. Negative values are not permitted.

Examples:

```
div#footer {max-height: 3em;}
```

max-width

Values:

<length> | <percentage> | none | inherit

Initial value: none

Applies to: All elements except inline nonreplaced elements and table elements.

Inherited: No.

Percentages: Refer to the height of the containing block.

Computed value: For percentages, as specified; for length values, the absolute length; otherwise, none.

Description:

The value of this property sets a maximum constraint on the width of the element. Thus, the element can be narrower than the specified value, but not wider. Negative values are not permitted.

Examples:

```
#sidebar img {width: 50px; max-width: 100%;}
```

min-height

Values:

<length> | <percentage> | `inherit`

Initial value:	0
Applies to:	All elements except inline nonreplaced elements and table elements.
Inherited:	No.
Percentages:	Refer to the width of the containing block.
Computed value:	For percentages, as specified; for length values, the absolute length.

Description:

The value of this property sets a minimum constraint on the height of the element. Thus, the element can be taller than the specified value, but not shorter. Negative values are not permitted.

Examples:

```
div#footer {min-height: 1em;}
```

min-width

Values:

<length> | <percentage> | `inherit`

Initial value: 0

Applies to: All elements except inline nonreplaced elements and table elements.

Inherited: No.

Percentages: Refer to the width of the containing block.

Computed value: For percentages, as specified; for length values, the absolute length; otherwise, none.

Description:

The value of this property sets a minimum constraint on the width of the element. Thus, the element can be wider than the specified value, but not narrower. Negative values are not permitted.

Examples:

```
div.aside {float: right; width: 13em; max-width: 33%;}
```

outline

Values:

[<outline-color> || <outline-style> || <outline-width>] | inherit

Initial value: Not defined for shorthand properties.

Applies to: All elements.

Inherited: No.

Computed value: See individual properties (`outline-color`, etc.).

Description:

This shorthand property is used to set the overall outline for an element. Outlines can be of irregular shape, and they do not change or otherwise affect the placement of elements.

Examples:

```
*[href]:focurs {outline: 2px dashed invert;}
form:focus {outline: outset cyan 0.25em;}
```

outline-color

Values:

<color> | invert | inherit

Initial value: invert (see Description, below)

Applies to: All elements.

Inherited: No.

Computed value: As specified.

Description:

This property sets the color for the visible portions of the overall outline of an element. Remember that an outline's style must be something other than none for any visible border to appear. User agents are permitted to ignore invert on platforms that don't support color inversion. In that case, the default is the value of color for the element.

Examples:

```
*[href]:focurs {outline-color: invert;}
form:focus {outline-color: cyan;}
```

outline-style

Values:

none | dotted | dashed | solid | double | groove | ridge | inset | outset | inherit

Initial value: none

Applies to: All elements

Inherited: No.

Computed value: As specified.

Description:

This property is used to set the style for the overall border of an element. The style must be something other than `none` for any outline to appear.

Examples:

```
*[href]:focus {outline-style: dashed;}
form:focus {outline-style: outset;}
```

outline-width

Values:

`thin` | `medium` | `thick` | <length> | `inherit`

Initial value: `medium`

Applies to: All elements.

Inherited: No.

Computed value: Absolute length; `0` if the style of the border is `none` or `hidden`.

Description:

This property sets the width for the overall outline of an element. The width will take effect only for a given outline if the outline's style is something other than `none`. If the style is `none`, then the width is effectively reset to `0`. Negative length values are not permitted.

Examples:

```
*[href]:focus {outline-width: 2px;}
form:focus {outline-width: 0.25em;}
```

overflow

Values:

`visible` | `hidden` | `scroll` | `auto` | `inherit`

Initial value: `visible`

Applies to: Block-level and replaced elements.

Inherited: No.

Computed value: As specified.

Description:

This defines what happens to content that overflows the content area of an element. For the value `scroll`, user agents should provide a scrolling mechanism whether or not it is actually needed; thus, for example, scrollbars would appear even if all content is able to fit within the element box.

Examples:

```
#masthead {overflow: hidden;}
object {overflow: scroll;}
```

---

padding

Values:

[<length> | <percentage>]{1,4} | `inherit`

Initial value: Not defined for shorthand elements.

Applies to: All elements.

Inherited: No.

Percentages: Refer to the width of the containing block.

Computed value: See individual properties (`padding-top`, etc.).

Note: Padding can never be negative.

Description:

This shorthand property sets the width of the overall padding for an element or sets the widths of each individual side padding. Padding set on inline nonreplaced elements does not affect line-height calculations; therefore, such an element with both padding and a background may visibly extend into other lines and potentially overlap other content. The background of the element will extend throughout the padding. Negative padding values are not permitted.

Examples:

```
h1 {padding: 2ex;}
img {padding: 10px;}
```

padding-bottom

Values:

<length> | <percentage> | `inherit`

Initial value: `0`

Applies to: All elements.

Inherited: No.

Percentages: Refer to the width of the containing block.

Computed value: For percentage values, as specified; for length values, the absolute length.

Note:

Padding can never be negative.

Description:

This property sets the width of the bottom padding for an element. Bottom padding set on inline nonreplaced elements does not affect line-height calculations; therefore, such an element with both bottom padding and a background may visibly extend into other lines and potentially overlap other content. Negative padding values are not permitted.

Examples:

```
ul {padding-bottom: 0.5in;}
h1 {padding-bottom: 2%;}
```

padding-left

Values:

<length> | <percentage> | `inherit`

Initial value: 0

Applies to: All elements.

Inherited: No.

Percentages: Refer to the width of the containing block.

Computed value: For percentage values, as specified; for length values, the absolute length.

Note: Padding can never be negative.

Description:

This property sets the width of the left padding for an element. Left padding set for an inline nonreplaced element will appear only on the left edge of the first inline box generated by the element. Negative padding values are not permitted.

Examples:

```
p {padding-left: 5%;}
pre {padding-left: 3em;}
```

padding-right

Values:

<length> | <percentage> | `inherit`

Initial value: 0

Applies to: All elements.

Inherited: No.

Percentages: Refer to the width of the containing block.

Computed value: For percentage values, as specified; for length values, the absolute length.

Note:

Padding can never be negative.

Description:

This property sets the width of the right padding for an element. Right padding set for an inline nonreplaced element will appear only on the right edge of the last inline box generated by the element. Negative padding values are not permitted.

Examples:

```
img {padding-right: 30px;}
ol {padding-right: 5em;}
```

padding-top

Values:

<length> | <percentage> | `inherit`

Initial value: `0`

Applies to: All elements.

Inherited: No.

Percentages: Refer to the width of the containing block.

Computed value: For percentage values, as specified; for length values, the absolute length.

Note:

Padding can never be negative.

Description:

This property sets the width of the top padding for an element. Top padding set on inline nonreplaced elements does not affect line-height calculations; therefore, such an element with both top padding and a background may visibly extend into other lines and potentially overlap other content. Negative padding values are not permitted.

Examples:

```
ul {padding-top: 0.5in;}
h3 {padding-top: 1.5em;}
```

position

Values:

`static` | `relative` | `absolute` | `fixed` | `inherit`

Initial value: `static`

Applies to: All elements.

Inherited: No.

Computed value: As specified.

Description:

This defines the positioning scheme used to lay out an element. Any element may be positioned, although elements positioned with `absolute` or `fixed` will generate a block-level box no matter what kind of element it is. An element that is relatively positioned is offset from its default placement in the normal flow.

Examples:

```
#footer {position: fixed; bottom: 0;}
*.offset {position: relative; top: 0.5em;}
```

quotes

Values:

[<string> <string>]+ | `none` | `inherit`

Initial value: User agent–dependent.

Applies to: All elements.

Inherited: Yes.

Computed value: As specified.

Description:

This property is used to determine the quotation pattern used with quotes and nested quotes. The actual quote marks are inserted via the property `content`.

Examples:

```
q {quotes: '\201C' '\201D' '\2018' '\2019';}
```

right

Values:

<length> | <percentage> | `auto` | `inherit`

Initial value: `auto`

Applies to: Positioned elements (that is, elements for which the value of `position` is something other than `static`).

Inherited: No.

Percentages: Refer to the width of the containing block.

Computed value:

For relatively positioned elements, see the following note; for `static` elements, auto; for length values, the corresponding absolute length; for percentage values, the specified value; otherwise, `auto`.

Note:

For relatively positioned elements, the computed value of `left` always equals `right`.

Description:

This property defines the offset between the right outer margin edge of a positioned element and the right edge of its containing block.

Examples:

```
div#footer {position: fixed; right: 0;}
*.overlapper {position: relative; right: -25px;}
```

---

text-align

CSS2.1values:

left | center | right | justify | inherit

CSS2 values:

left | center | right | justify | <string> | inherit

Initial value: User agent–specific; may also depend on writing direction.

Applies to: Block-level elements.

Inherited: Yes.

Computed value: As specified.

Note:

CSS2 included a <string> value that was dropped from CSS2.1 due to a lack of support.

Description:

This property sets the horizontal alignment of text within a block-level element by defining the point to which line boxes are aligned. The value justify is supported by allowing user agents to programmatically adjust the letter and word spacing of the line's content; results may vary by user agent.

Examples:

```
p {text-align: justify;}
h4 {text-align: center;}
```

text-decoration

Values:

`none` | [`underline` || `overline` || `line-through` || `blink`] | `inherit`

Initial value: `none`

Applies to: All elements.

Inherited: No.

Computed value: As specified.

Description:

This property allows certain text effects such as underlining. These decorations will span descendant elements that do not have decorations of their own. User agents are not required to support `blink`. These decorations will span child elements which do not have text decoration defined; see Chapter 6 of *Cascading Style Sheets: The Definitive Guide*, Second Edition (O'Reilly), for more details. Combinations of the values are legal. Any time two `text-decoration` declarations apply to the same element, the values of the two declarations are *not* combined. For example:

```
h1 {text-decoration: overline;}
h1, h2 {text-decoration: underline;}
```

Given these styles, `h1` elements will be underlined with no overline, because the value of `overline` completely overrides the value of `underline`. If `h1`s should have both overlines and underlines, then use the value `overline underline` for the `h1` rule.

Examples:

```
u {text-decoration: underline;}
.old {text-decoration: line-through;}
u.old {text-decoration: line-through underline;}
```

text-indent

Values:

<length> | <percentage> | `inherit`

Initial value: 0

Applies to: Block-level elements.

Inherited: Yes.

Percentages: Refer to the width of the containing block.

Computed value: For percentage values, as specified; for length values, the absolute length.

Description:

Used to define the indentation of the first line of content in a block-level element. This is most often used to create a tab effect. Negative values are permitted and cause outdent (or hanging indent) effects.

Examples:

```
p {text-indent: 5em;}
h2 {text-indent: -25px;}
```

text-transform

Values:

`uppercase` | `lowercase` | `capitalize` | `none` | `inherit`

Initial value: none

Applies to: All elements.

Inherited: Yes.

Computed value: As specified.

Description:

This property changes the case of letters in an element, regardless of the case of the text in the document source. The determination of which letters are to be capitalized by the value `capitalize` is not precisely defined, as it depends on user agents knowing how to recognize a "word."

Examples:

```
h1 {text-transform: uppercase;}
.title {text-transform: capitalize;}
```

top

Values:

<length> | <percentage> | `auto` | `inherit`

Initial value: `auto`

Applies to: Positioned elements (that is, elements for which the value of `position` is something other than `static`).

Inherited: No.

Percentages: Refer to the height of the containing block.

Computed value: For relatively positioned elements, see note; for `static` elements, `auto`; for length values, the corresponding absolute length; for percentage values, the specified value; otherwise, `auto`.

Note:

For relatively positioned elements, if both `top` and `bottom` are `auto`, their computed values are both `0`; if one of them is `auto`, it becomes the negative of the other; if neither is `auto`, `bottom` will become the negative of the value of `top`.

Description:

This property defines the offset between the top outer margin edge of a positioned element and the top edge of its containing block.

Examples:

```
#masthead {position: fixed; top: 0;}
sub {position: relative; top: 0.5em; vertical-align:
baseline;}
```

unicode-bidi

Values:

`normal` | `embed` | `bidi-override` | `inherit`

Initial value: `normal`

Applies to: All elements.

Inherited: No.

Computed value: As specified.

Description:

Allows the author to generate levels of embedding within the Unicode embedding algorithm. User agents that do not support bidirectional text are permitted to ignore this property.

Examples:

```
*:lang(ar) {direction: rtl; unicode-bidi: embed;}
*:lang(es) {direction: ltr; unicode-bidi: normal;}
```

vertical-align

Values:

`baseline` | `sub` | `super` | `top` | `text-top` | `middle` | `bottom` | `text-bottom` | <percentage> | <length> | `inherit`

Initial value: `baseline`

Applies to: Inline elements and table cells.

Inherited: No.

Percentages: Refer to the value of `line-height` for the element.

Computed value: For percentage and length values, the absolute length; otherwise, as specified.

Note:

When applied to table cells, only the values `baseline`, `top`, `middle`, and `bottom` are recognized.

Description:

This defines the vertical alignment of an inline element's baseline with respect to the baseline of the line in which it resides. Negative length and percentage values are permitted, and they lower the element instead of raising it. In table cells, this property sets the alignment of the content of the cell within the cell box.

Examples:

```
sup {vertical-align: super;}
.fnote {vertical-align: 50%;}
```

visibility

Values:

`visible` | `hidden` | `collapse` | `inherit`

Initial value: `inherit`

Applies to: All elements.

Inherited: No.

Computed value: As specified.

Description:

This specifies whether the element box generated by an element is rendered. This means authors can have the element take up the space it would ordinarily take up while remaining completely invisible. The value `collapse` is used in tables to remove columns or rows from the table's layout.

Examples:

```
ul.submenu {visibility: hidden;}
tr.hide {visibility: collapse;}
```

white-space

Values:

`normal` | `nowrap` | `pre` | `pre-wrap` | `pre-line` | `inherit`

Initial value: `normal`

Applies to: All elements (CSS2.1); block-level elements (CSS2).

Inherited: No.

Computed value: As specified.

Description:

This declares how whitespace within an element is handled during layout. `normal` acts like traditional web browsers, in that it reduces any sequence of whitespace to a single space. `pre` causes whitespace to be treated as it is in the HTML element PRE, with whitespace and returns fully preserved. `nowrap` prevents an element from line-breaking, as in the "nowrap" attribute for TD and TH elements in HTML4. The values `pre-wrap` and `pre-line` were added in CSS2.1; the former causes the user agent to preserve whitespace while still automatically wrapping lines of text, and the latter honors newline characters within the text while collapsing all other whitespace as per `normal`.

Examples:

```
td {white-space: nowrap;}
tt {white-space: pre;}
```

width

Values:

<length> | <percentage> | `auto` | `inherit`

Initial value: `auto`

Applies to: Block-level and replaced elements.

Inherited: No.

Percentages: Refer to the width of the containing block.

Computed value: For `auto` and percentage values, as specified; otherwise, an absolute length, unless the property does not apply to the element (then `auto`).

Description:

This defines the width of an element's content area, outside of which padding, borders, and margins are added. This property is ignored for inline nonreplaced elements. Negative length and percentage values are not permitted.

Examples:

```
table {width: 80%;}
#sidebar {width: 20%;}
.figure img {width: 200px;}
```

word-spacing

Values:

<length> | `normal` | `inherit`

Initial value: `normal`

Applies to: All elements.

Inherited: Yes.

Computed value: For `normal`, the absolute length `0`; otherwise, the absolute length.

Description:

This defines the amount of whitespace to be inserted between words in an element. For the purposes of this property, a word is defined to be a string of characters surrounded by whitespace. Length values create a modifier to the usual spacing between words; thus, `normal` is synonymous with `0`. Negative length values are permitted and will cause words to bunch closer together.

Examples:

```
p.spacious {word-spacing: 0.5em;}
em {word-spacing: 5px;}
p.cramped {word-spacing: -0.2em;}
```

z-index

Values:

<integer> | `auto` | `inherit`

Initial value: `auto`

Applies to: Positioned elements.

Inherited: No.

Computed value: As specified.

Description:

This property sets the placement of a positioned element along the z-axis, which is defined to be the axis that extends perpendicular to the display area. Positive numbers are closer to the user, and negative numbers are further away.

Examples:

```
#masthead {position: relative; z-index: 10000;}
```

Tables

border-collapse

Values:

`collapse` | `separate` | `inherit`

Initial value: `separate`

Applies to: Elements with the `display` value `table` or `table-inline`.

Inherited: Yes.

Computed value: As specified.

Note:

In CSS2, the default value was `collapse`.

Description:

This property is used to define the layout model used in laying out the borders in a table—i.e., those applied to cells, rows, and so forth. Although the property applies only to tables, it is inherited by all the elements within the table.

Examples:

```
table {border-collapse: separate; border-spacing: 3px 5px;}
```

border-spacing

Values:

<length> <length>? | `inherit`

Initial value: `0`

Applies to: Elements with the `display` value `table` or `table-inline`.

Inherited: Yes.

Computed value: Two absolute lengths.

Note:

Property is ignored unless `border-collapse` value is `separate`.

Description:

This specifies the distance between cell borders in the separated borders model. The first of the two length values is the horizontal separation and the second is the vertical. This property is ignored unless `border-collapse` is set to `separate`. Although the property only applies to tables, it is inherited by all of the elements within the table.

Examples:

```
table {border-collapse: separate; border-spacing: 0;}
table {border-collapse: separate; border-spacing: 3px 5px;}
```

caption-side

Values:

`top` | `bottom`

Initial value: `top`

Applies to: Elements with the `display` value `table-caption`.

Inherited: No.

Computed value: As specified.

Note:

The values `left` and `right` appeared in CSS2 but were dropped from CSS2.1 due to a lack of widespread support.

Description:

This specifies the placement of a table caption with respect to the table box. The caption is rendered as though it were a block-level element placed just before (or after) the table.

Examples:

```
caption {caption-side: top;}
```

empty-cells

Values:

`show` | `hide` | `inherit`

Initial value: `show`

Applies to: Elements with the `display` value `table-cell`.

Inherited: Yes.

Computed value: As specified.

Note:

Property is ignored unless `border-collapse` value is `separate`.

Description:

This defines the presentation of table cells that contain no content. If shown, the cell's borders and background are drawn. This property is ignored unless `border-collapse` is set to `separate`.

Examples:

```
th, td {empty-cells: show;}
```

table-layout

Values:

`auto` | `fixed` | `inherit`

Initial value: `auto`

Applies to: Elements with the `display` value `table` or `inline-table`.

Inherited: Yes.

Computed value: As specified.

Description:

This property is used to specify which layout algorithm is used to lay out a table. The fixed layout algorithm is faster but less flexible, while the automatic algorithm is slower but more reflective of traditional HTML tables.

Examples:

```
table.fast {table-layout: fixed;}
```

Paged Media

orphans

Values:

<integer> | inherit

Initial value: 2

Applies to: Block-level elements.

Inherited: Yes.

Computed value: As specified.

Description:

This specifies the minimum number of text lines within the element that can be left at the bottom of a page. This can affect the placement of page breaks within the element.

Examples:

```
p {orhpans: 4;}
ul {orphans: 2;}
```

page-break-after

Values:

auto | always | avoid | left | right | inherit

Initial value: auto

Applies to: Nonfloated block-level elements with a position value of relative or static.

Inherited: No.

Computed value: As specified.

Description:

This declares whether page breaks should be placed after an element. While it is possible to force breaks with `always`, it is not possible to guarantee prevention; `avoid` asks the user agent to avoid inserting a page break if possible.

Examples:

```
div.section {page-break-after: always;}
h2 {page-break-after: avoid;}
```

page-break-before

Values:

`auto` | `always` | `avoid` | `left` | `right` | `inherit`

Initial value: `auto`

Applies to: Nonfloated block-level elements with a `position` value of `relative` or `static`.

Inherited: No.

Computed value: As specified.

Description:

Declares whether page breaks should be placed before an element. While it is possible to force breaks with `always`, it is not possible to guarantee prevention; the best an author can do is ask the user agent to avoid inserting a page break if possible.

Examples:

```
p + ul {page-break-before: avoid;}
h2 {page-break-before: always;}
```

page-break-inside

Values:

`auto` | `avoid` | `inherit`

Initial value: `auto`

Applies to: Nonfloated block-level elements with a `position` value of `relative` or `static`.

Inherited: Yes.

Computed value: As specified.

Description:

This declares whether page breaks should be placed inside an element. Because an element might be taller than a page box, it is not possible to guarantee prevention; the best an author can do is ask the user agent to `avoid` inserting a page break if possible.

Examples:

```
table {page-break-inside: avoid;}
```

widows

Values:

<integer> | `inherit`

Initial value: `2`

Applies to: Block-level elements.

Inherited: Yes.

Computed value: As specified.

Description:

This specifies the minimum number of text lines within the element that can be left at the top of a page. This can affect the placement of page breaks within the element.

Examples:

```
p {widows: 4;}
ul {widows: 2;}
```

Dropped from CSS2.1

The following properties appeared in CSS2 but were dropped from CSS2.1 due to a lack of widespread support. They do not have computed value information, since computed values were first explicitly defined in CSS2.1.

Visual Styles

font-size-adjust

Values:

<number> | `none` | `inherit`

Initial value: `none`

Applies to: All elements.

Inherited: Yes.

Description:

The aim of this property is to allow authors to trigger font scaling such that substitute fonts will not look too wildly different from the font the author wanted to use, even if the substituted font has a different x-height. Note that this property does not appear in CSS2.1.

font-stretch

Values:

`normal` | `wider` | `narrower` | `ultra-condensed` | `extra-condensed` | `condensed` | `semi-condensed` | `semi-expanded` | `expanded` | `extra-expanded` | `ultra-expanded` | `inherit`

Initial value: `normal`

Applies to: All elements.

Inherited: Yes.

Description:

With this property, the character glyphs in a given font can be made wider or narrower, ideally by selected condensed or expanded faces from the font's family. Note that this property does not appear in CSS2.1.

marker-offset

Values:

<length> | `auto` | `inherit`

Initial value: `auto`

Applies to: Elements with a `display` value of `marker`.

Inherited: No.

Note:

This property is obsolete as of CSS2.1 and will likely not appear in CSS3, with the same holding true for the `display` value of `marker`; as of this writing, it appears that other mechanisms will be used to achieve these effects.

Description:

This property specifies the distance between the nearest border edge of a marker box and its associated element box.

text-shadow

Values:

none | [<color> || <length> <length> <length>? ,]* [<color> || <length> <length> <length>?] | `inherit`

Initial value: none

Applies to: All elements.

Inherited: No.

Description:

This permits the assignments of one or more "shadows" to the text in an element. The first two length values in a shadow definition set horizontal and vertical offsets, respectively, from the element's text. The third length defines a blurring radius. Note that this property does not appear in CSS2.1.

Paged Media

marks

Values:

[`crop` || `cross`] | `none` | `inherit`

Initial value: `none`

Applies to: Page context.

Inherited: N/A.

Description:

This property defines whether "cross marks" (otherwise known as register marks or registration marks) should be placed outside the content area but within the printable area of the canvas. The exact placement and rendering of the marks is not defined. Note that this value does not appear in CSS2.1.

page

Values:

<identifier> | `inherit`

Initial value: `auto`

Applies to: Block-level elements.

Inherited: Yes.

Description:

This property, in conjunction with `size`, specifies a particular page type to be used in the printing of an element. Note that this property does not appear in CSS2.1.

size

Values:

<length>{1,2} | `auto` | `portrait` | `landscape` | `inherit`

Initial value: `auto`

Applies to: The page area.

Inherited: No.

Description:

With this property, authors can declare the size and orientation of the page box used in the printing of an element. It can be used in conjunction with page, although this is not always necessary. Note that this property does not appear in CSS2.1.

Aural Styles

azimuth

Values:

<angle> | [[`left-side` | `far-left` | `left` | `center-left` | `center` | `center-right` | `right` | `far-right` | `right-side`] || `behind`] | `leftwards` | `rightwards` | `inherit`

Initial value: `center`

Applies to: All elements.

Inherited: Yes.

Computed value: Normalized angle.

Description:

This property sets the angle along the horizontal plane (otherwise known as the horizon) from which a sound should seem to emanate. This is used in conjunction with `elevation` to place the sound at a point on a hypothetical sphere with the user at its center.

---

cue

Values:

[<cue-before> || <cue-after>] | `inherit`

Initial value: none

Applies to: All elements.

Inherited: No.

Computed value: See individual properties (`cue-before`, etc.).

Description:

This is a shorthand property that allows an author to define cues that precede and follow the audio rendering of an element's content. A cue is something like an auditory icon.

---

cue-after

Values:

<uri> | none | `inherit`

Initial value: none

Applies to: All elements.

Inherited: No.

Computed value: For <uri> values, the absolute URI; otherwise, none.

Description:

This property allows an author to define a cue that follows the audio rendering of an element's content.

---

cue-before

Values:

<uri> | `none` | `inherit`

Initial value: `none`

Applies to: All elements.

Inherited: No.

Computed value: For <uri> values, the absolute URI; otherwise, `none`.

Description:

This property allows an author to define a cue that precedes the audio rendering of an element's content.

---

elevation

Values:

<angle> | `below` | `level` | `above` | `higher` | `lower` | `inherit`

Initial value: `level`

Applies to: All elements.

Inherited: Yes.

Computed value: Normalized angle.

Description:

This property sets the angle above or below the horizontal plane (otherwise known as the horizon) from which a sound should seem to emanate. This is used in conjunction with `azimuth` to place the sound at a point on a hypothetical sphere with the user at its center.

pause

Values:

[[<time> | <percentage>]{1,2}] | `inherit`

Initial value: 0

Applies to: All elements.

Inherited: No.

Computed value: See individual properties (`pause-before`, etc.).

Description:

This is a shorthand property that allows an author to define pauses that precede and follow the audio rendering of an element's content. A pause is an interval in which no content is audibly rendered, although background sounds may still be audible.

pause-after

Values:

<time> | <percentage> | `inherit`

Initial value:s: 0

Applies to: All elements.

Inherited: No.

Computed value: The absolute time value.

Description:

This property allows an author to define the length of a pause that follows the audio rendering of an element's content.

pause-before

Values:

<time> | <percentage> | `inherit`

Initial value: `0`

Applies to: All elements.

Inherited: No.

Computed value: The absolute time value.

Description:

This property allows an author to define the length of a pause that precedes the audio rendering of an element's content.

pitch

Values:

<frequency> | `x-low` | `low` | `medium` | `high` | `x-high` | `inherit`

Initial value: `medium`

Applies to: All elements.

Inherited: Yes.

Computed value: The absolute frequency value.

Description:

Specifies the average pitch (frequency) of the speaking voice used to audibly render the element's content. The average pitch of a voice will depend greatly on the voice family.

pitch-range

Values:

<number> | `inherit`

Initial value: 50

Applies to: All elements.

Inherited: Yes.

Computed value: As specified.

Description:

This property specifies the variation in average pitch used by the speaking voice, while audibly rendering the element's content. The higher the variation, the more animated the voice will sound.

play-during

Values:

<uri> | [`mix` || `repeat`]? | `auto` | `none` | `inherit`

Initial value: `auto`

Applies to: All elements.

Inherited: No.

Computed value:

For <uri> values, the absolute URI; otherwise, as specified.

Description:

This provides a sound to be played in the background while the element's contents are audibly rendered. The sound can be mixed with other background sounds (set using `play-during` on an ancestor element), or it can replace other sounds for the duration of the element's audio rendering.

richness

Values:

<number> | `inherit`

Initial value: 50

Applies to: All elements.

Inherited: Yes.

Computed value: As specified.

Description:

This property sets the brightness of the speaking voice used when audibly rendering the element's content. The brighter the voice, the more it will carry.

speak

Values:

`normal` | `none` | `spell-out` | `inherit`

Initial value: `normal`

Applies to: All elements.

Inherited: Yes.

Computed value: As specified.

Description:

This determines how an element's contents will be audibly rendered, or if they will be rendered at all. The value `spell-out` is typically used for acronyms and abbreviations such as W3C or CSS. If the value is `none`, then the element is skipped (it takes no time to be audibly rendered).

speak-header

Values:

`once` | `always` | `inherit`

Initial value: `once`

Applies to: Elements containing table header information.

Inherited: Yes.

Computed value: As specified.

Description:

This specifies whether the content of table headers is spoken before every cell associated with those headers, or only when the header associated with a cell is different than the header associated with the previously rendered cell.

speak-numeral

Values:

`digits` | `continuous` | `inherit`

Initial value: `continuous`

Applies to: All elements.

Inherited: Yes.

Computed value: As specified.

Description:

This property determines how numbers are spoken during audible rendering.

speak-punctuation

Values:

`code` | `none` | `inherit`

Initial value: `none`

Applies to: All elements.

Inherited: Yes.

Computed value: As specified.

Description:

This property determines how punctuation is spoken during audible rendering. The value code causes punctuation symbols to be rendered literally.

speech-rate

Values:

<number> | `x-slow` | `slow` | `medium` | `fast` | `x-fast` | `faster`| `slower` | `inherit`

Initial value: `medium`

Applies to: All elements.

Inherited: Yes.

Computed value: An absolute number.

Description:

This sets the average rate at which words are spoken when an element's content is audibly rendered.

stress

Values:

<number> | `inherit`

Initial value: `50`

Applies to: All elements.

Inherited: Yes.

Computed value: As specified.

Description:

This property affects the height of peaks in the intonation of a speaking voice. These peaks are in turn generated by stress marks within a language.

voice-family

Values:

[[<specific-voice> | <generic-voice>],]* [<specific-voice> | <generic-voice>] | `inherit`

Initial value: User agent–dependent.

Applies to: All elements.

Inherited: Yes.

Computed value: As specified.

Description:

This property is used to define a list of voice families that can be used in the audio rendering of an element's content, and is comparable to `font-family`. The permitted generic voices are `male`, `female`, and `child`.

volume

Values:

<number> | <percentage> | `silent` | `x-soft` | `soft` | `medium`| `loud` | `x-loud` | `inherit`

Initial value: `medium`

Applies to: All elements.

Inherited: Yes.

Computed value: An absolute number.

Description:

This sets the median volume level for the waveform of the audibly rendered content. Thus, a waveform with large peaks and valleys may go well above or below the volume level set with this property. Note that `0` is not the same as `silent`.

Index

A

B

We'd like to hear your suggestions for improving our indexes. Send email to *index@oreilly.com*.

Shroff / O'Reilly

TITLES AT REDUCED PRICES

ISBN	Title	Author	Price
8173663661	.NET Framework Essentials, *324 Pages*	Thai	75.00
818404027X	**Access 2003 for Starters: The Missing Manual, *408 Pages***	**Chase**	**75.00**
8173664277	Access Cookbook for 97, 2000 & 2002 **(Book / CD-ROM)**, *724 Pages*	Getz	100.00
8173662231	ActionScriprt: The Definitive Guide, *726 Pages*	Moock	150.00
8173662886	Building Oracle XML Applications **(Book / CD-ROM)**, *824 Pages*	Muench	100.00
8173665621	**Building Secure Servers with Linux, *454 Pages***	**Bauer**	**100.00**
8173664250	Building Wireless Community Networks, *144 Pages*	Flickenger	50.00
8173662584	Cascading Style Sheets: The Definitive Guide, *476 Pages*	Meyer	75.00
8173669066	**Cascading Style Sheets: The Definitive Guide (Covers CSS2 & CSS 2.1), 2/ed, *538 Pages***	**Meyer**	**100.00**
8173667241	**Cisco Cookbook, *918 Pages***	**Dooley**	**150.00**
8173662878	Developing ASP Components 2/ed, *864 Pages*	Powers	100.00
8173663882	**Designing Large Scale LANs, *408 Pages***	**Dooley**	**75.00**
817366272X	DHCP for Windows 2000, *288 Pages*	Alcott	75.00
8173663599	Exim: The Mail Transport Agent, *638 Pages*	Hazel	75.00
8173663580	**Essential SNMP, *338 Pages***	**Mauro**	**75.00**
8173662754	**Excel 2000 In a Nutshell: A Power User's Quick Reference, *560 Pages***	**Simon**	**50.00**
8173669406	**Excel Annoyances: How to Fix the Most Annoying Things about Your Favorite Spreadsheet , *266 Pages***	**Frye**	**75.0**
8173668612	**Excel Hacks: 100 Industrial Strength Tips & Tools, *316 Pages***	**David**	**75.00**
8173669325	**Google: The Missing Manual, *312 Pages***	**Milstein**	**75.00**
8173663246	**Oracle Net8 Configuration & Troubleshooting, *412 Pages***	**Toledo**	**75.00**
8173660573	Java Threads, 2/ed, *336 Pages*	Oaks	100.00
8173664145	Java Cookbook, *890 Pages*	Darwin	150.00
8173664625	**Java Enterprise in a Nutshell: A Desktop Quick Reference, 2/ed, *1,004 Pages***	**Farley**	**100.00**
8173660557	Java Foundation Classes in a Nutshell, *752 Pages*	Flanagan	75.00
8173662711	Java Internationalization, *456 Pages*	Deitsch	75.00
8173663807	Java Programming with Oracle SQLJ, *404 Pages*	Price	75.00
8173661103	JavaScript Application Cookbook, *512 Pages*	Bradenbaugh	75.00
8173661111	JavaScript Pocket Reference, *96 Pages*	Flanagan	25.00
8173662500	Jini in a Nutshell, *420 Pages*	Oaks	75.00
8173665168	**Learning C#, *374 Pages***	**Liberty**	**75.00**
8173662320	Learning Java **(Book / CD-ROM)**, *732 Pages*	Niemeyer	75.00
8173660603	Learning Perl/Tk, *380 Pages*	Walsh	75.00
8173661677	Learning Web Design: A Beginner's Guide to HTML, Graphics & Web Environment (2 Color Book), *432 Pages*	Niederst	100.00
8173663173	Learning WML & WMLScript, *204 Pages*	Frost	50.00
8173663149	Learning XML, *376 Pages*	Ray	75.00
8173662193	MCSD in a Nutshell: The Visual Basic Exams, *636 Pages*	Foxall	75.00
8173662398	MCSE in a Nutshell: The Windows 2000 Exams, *504 Pages*	Moncur	75.00
8173662517	MP3: The Definitive Guide, *408 Pages*	Hacker	75.00
817366448X	**IPv6 Essentials, *362 Pages***	**Hagen**	**75.00**
8173665613	**Object-Oriented Programming with Visual Basic .NET, *306 Pgs***	**Hamilton**	**50.00**
8173660697	Oracle PL/SQL Language Pocket Reference, *80 Pages*	Feuerstein	25.00
8173667195	**Perl 6 Essentials, *208 Pages***	**Randal**	**75.00**

ISBN	Title	Author	Price
8173661243	Perl/Tk Pocket Reference, *104 Pages*	Lidie	25.00
817366269X	PHP Pocket Reference, *124 Pages*	Lerdorf	25.00
8173661251	PNG: The Definitive Guide, *344 Pages*	Roelofs	50.00
817366126X	Practical Internet Groupware, *520 Pages*	Udell	75.00
8173660751	Practical UNIX & Internet Security, 2/ed, *1,008 Pages*	Garfinkel	150.00
8173660190	QuarkXPress in a Nutshell, *552 Pages*	O'Quinn	50.00
8173662487	sed & awk Pocket Reference, *60 Pages*	Robbins	25.00
8173661294	sendmail Desktop Reference, *74 Pages*	Costales	25.00
8173662924	**SSH: The Secure Shell: The Definitive Guide, *564 Pages***	**Barrett**	**75.00**
8173664161	**Server Load Balancing,*198 Pages***	**Bourke**	**50.00**
8173663866	**Solaris 8 Administrator's Guide, *308 Pages***	**Watters**	**100.00**
8173662606	Tcl/Tk Pocket Reference, *100 Pages*	Raines	25.00
8173664374	**VB .NET Core Classes in a Nutshell: A Desktop Quick Reference (Book / CD-ROM), *584 Pages***	**Kurniawan**	**75.00**
817366501X	**Visual Studio Hacks: Tips & Tools for Turbocharging the IDE, *304 Pages***	**Avery**	**75.00**
8173663475	Web Database Applications with PHP & MySQL, *600 Pages*	Williams	75.00
8173665931	**WebLogic Server 6.1 Workbook for Enterprise JavaBeans, 3/ed, *264 Pages***	**Nyberg**	**50.00**
8173662770	**Word 2000 in a Nutshell: A Power User's Quick Reference, *516 Pages***	**Glenn**	**50.00**
8173666113	**Word Annoyances, *218 Pages***	**Hart**	**75.00**
8173661359	Webmaster in a Nutshell, 2/ed, *540 Pages*	Spainhour	75.00
8173662630	Windows 2000 Active Directory, *624 Pages*	Lowe-Norris	75.00
8173662789	**Windows 2000 Administration in a Nutshell: A Desktop Quick Reference, *1000 Pages***	**Tulloch**	**50.00**
8173663327	Windows 2000 Performance Guide, *650 Pages*	Friedman	75.00
8173660743	**Windows 2000 Quick Fixes, *304 Pages***	**Boyce**	**50.00**
8173666903	**Windows Server 2003 in a Nutshell: A Desktop Quick Reference, *672 Pages***	**Tulloch**	**75.00**
8173663564	**Windows XP in a Nutshell: A Desktop Quick Reference, *640 Pages***	**Karp**	**75.00**
8173665915	**Windows XP Unwired: A Guide for Home, Office, and the Road, *316 Pages***	**Lee**	**75.00**
8173668086	**X Protocol Reference Manual (Version X11): Volume Zero, *468 Pages***	**Nye**	**75.00**
8173668094	**Xlib Programming Manual (Version 11): Volume One, *824 Pages***	**Nye**	**100.00**
8173668108	**Xlib Reference Manual (Version 11), 3/ed: Volume Two, *948 Pages***	**Nye**	**100.00**
8173662096	XSLT, *486 Pages*	Tidwell	100.00

PUBLISHED TITLES

8173666539	.NET and XML, *484 Pages*	Bornstein	425.00
8173669201	.NET Compact Framework Pocket Guide, *122 Pages*	Lee	125.00
8173666547	.NET Framework Essentials, 3/ed, *392 Pages*	Thai	325.00
8173665729	.NET Gotchas: 75 Ways to Improve Your C# and VB.NET Programs, *402 Pgs*	Subramaniam	300.00
8173665753	802.11 Security, *200 Pages*	Potter	175.00
8184041632	**802.11 Wireless Networks: The Definitive Guide, 2/ed, *668 Pages***	**Gast**	**600.00**
8173661995	**Access 2003 Personal Trainer (Book / CD-ROM), (2 Color book), *372 Pgs***	**CustomGuide**	**400.00**
8184042574	**Access 2007: The Missing Manual, *776 Pages***	**MacDonald**	**525.00**
8173664285	Access Database Design & Programming, 3/ed, *454 Pages*	Roman	325.00
8173666377	Access Hacks: Tips & Tools for Wrangling Your Data, *362 Pgs*	Bluttman	325.00

ISBN	Title	Author	Price
8184042833	**ActionScript 3.0 Cookbook, *600 Pages***	**Lott**	**475.00**
8173667233	ActionScript Cookbook, *904 Pages*	Lott	675.00
8173666555	ActionScript for Flash MX Pocket Reference, *152 Pages*	Moock	125.00
8173665761	ActionScript for Flash MX: The Definitive Guide, 2/ed, *904 Pg*	Colin Moock	750.00
8173667357	Active Directory Cookbook for Windows Server 2003 and Windows 2000, *632 Pages*	Allen	525.00
8173666563	Active Directory for Windows Server 2003, 2/ed, *692 Pages*	Allen	575.00
817366725X	ADO .NET Cookbook, *636 Pages*	Hamilton	500.00
8173665222	ADO .NET for Visual Basic .NET 2003 in a Nutshell: A Desktop Quick Reference **(Book / CD-ROM)**, *626 Pages*	Hamilton	500.00
0596102364	**Adobe Creative Suite 2 Workflow, *634 Pages***	**Alspach**	**1,625.00**
0596006004	Adobe Encore DVD: In the Studio, *336 Pages*	Dixon	1,225.00
0596100973	**Adobe InDesign CS2 One-on-One (Book / CD-ROM), *420 Pgs***	**McClelland**	**1,375.00**
0596100965	**Adobe Photoshop CS2 One-on-One (Book / DVD), *512 Pages***	**McClelland**	**1,225.00**
8173668302	Advanced Perl Programming, 2/ed, *308 Pages*	Cozens	325.00
8173668205	AI for Game Developers, *400 Pages*	Bourg	375.00
8184041578	**Ajax Design Patterns, *668 Pages***	**Mahemoff**	**500.00**
8184042612	**Ajax on Rails, *364 Pages***	**Raymond**	**350.00**
8184041063	**Ajax Hacks: Tips & Tools for Creating Responsive Web Sites, *304 Pages***	**Perry**	**350.00**
8184042701	**Astronomy Hacks, *420 Pages***	**Thompson**	**450.00**
8173667292	Amazon Hacks: 100 Industrial Strength Tips & Tricks, *312 Pages*	Bausch	250.00
8173667799	**Analyzing Business Data with Excel, *276 Pages***	**Knight**	**275.00**
8184040806	**ANT: The Definitive Guide, 2/ed (Cover ANT 1.6), *346 Pages***	**Holzner**	**325.00**
8173667446	Apache Cookbook (Covers Apache 2.0 & 1.3), *264 Pages*	Coar	250.00
8173662525	Apache Pocket Reference, *112 Pages*	Ford	75.00
8173662274	Apache Security, *428 Pages*	Ristic	400.00
8173665133	Apache: The Definitive Guide (Covers Apache 2.0 & 1.3) 3/ed, *594 Pages*	Laurie	500.00
8184040393	Applied Software Project Management, *304 Pages*	Stellman	350.00
8173667837	The Art of Project Management, *512 Pages*	Berkun	350.00
8184041411	**The Art of SQL, *382 Pages***	**Faroult**	**350.00**
8184041020	**ASP .NET 2.0 Cookbook (Cover ASP .NET 2.0), *1,028 Pages***	**Kittel**	**675.00**
8173664587	**ASP .NET 2.0: Developer's Notebook, *358 Pages***	**Lee**	**325.00**
8173667306	ASP .NET in a Nutshell: A Desktop Quick Reference, 2/ed, *1,008 Pages*	Duthie	600.00
8173669384	AspectJ Cookbook, *364 Pages*	Miles	350.00
8184040016	Asterisk: The Future of Telephony, *414 Pages*	Meggelen	375.00
8173662347	AutoCAD 2000 In a Nutshell: A Command Reference Guide, *592 Pgs*	Kent	325.00
8173663955	Beginning Perl for Bioinformatics, *390 Pages*	Tisdall	300.00
8173668981	Better, Faster, Lighter Java, *270 Pages*	Tate	250.00
8184040032	Beyond Java, *206 Pages*	Tate	200.00
817366658X	BGP, *292 Pages*	van Beijnum	275.00
8184040547	**Blackberry Hacks: Tips & Tools for Your Mobile Office, *350 Pgs***	**Mabe**	**350.00**
8173665125	BLAST, *372 Pages*	Korf	325.00
817366899X	BSD Hacks:100 Industrial-Strength Tips & Tools, *458 Pages*	Lavigne	375.00
8173666598	Building Embedded Linux Systems, *422 Pages*	Yaghmour	350.00
0596101368	**Building Extreme PCs, *192 Pages***	**Hardwidge**	**1,200.00**

ISBN	Title	Author	Price
8173661014	Building Internet Firewalls 2/ed, *904 Pages*	Chapman	650.00
8173662282	Building Java Enterprise Applications: Vol. 1 - Architecture, *324 Pages*	McLaughlin	225.00
8173661391	Building Linux Clusters **(Book / CD-ROM)**, *360 Pages*	Spector	350.00
8184041543	**Building Scalable Web Sites, *362 Pages***	**Henderson**	**325.00**
8173664749	**Building the Perfect PC, *360 Pages***	**Thompson**	**350.00**
8173664439	C# & VB .NET Conversion Pocket Reference, *156 Pages*	Mojica	75.00
8184040938	**C# Cookbook, 2/ed (Updated for C# 2.0 and .NET 2.0), *1,196 Pgs***	**Hilyard**	**600.00**
8173664293	C# Essentials, 2/ed, *224 Pages*	Albahari	175.00
8173663726	C# in a Nutshell: A Desktop Quick Reference, *864 Pages*	Drayton	600.00
8173665192	C# Language Pocket Reference, *132 Pages*	Drayton	100.00
8184040490	**C in a Nutshell, *618 Pages***	**Prinz**	**350.00**
8173666601	C Pocket Reference, *142 Pages*	Prinz	100.00
8184040369	**C++ Cookbook, *604 Pages***	**Stephens**	**400.00**
8173666628	C++ in a Nutshell, (Cover ISO/IEC 14882 STD) *816 Pages*	Lischner	500.00
8173667101	C++ Pocket Reference, *148 Pages*	Loudon	100.00
0596001088	The Cathedral & The Bazaar: Musings On Linux and Open Source by an Accidental Revolutionary, Revised & Expanded, *256 Pages*	Raymond	525.00
8173662266	CDO & MAPI Programming with Visual Basic, *388 Pages*	Grundgeiger	175.00
8173664269	CGI Programming on the World Wide Web, *454 Pages*	Gundavaram	300.00
817366045X	CGI Programming with Perl 2/ed, *476 Pages*	Gundavaram	350.00
8184042841	**Cisco IOS Cookbook 2/ed, *1250 Pages***	**Dooley**	**750.00**
8173669848	Cisco IOS in a Nutshell, 2/ed: A Desktop Quick Reference for IOS on IP Network, *808 Pages*	Boney	500.00
8173668469	Classic Shell Scripting, *568 Pages*	Robbins	425.00
8173663645	COM+ Programming with Visual Basic, *372 Pages*	Mojica	225.00
8173663653	COM & .NET Component Services, *390 Pages*	Lowy	250.00
059600849X	**Commercial Photoshop Retouching: In The Studio, *410 Pages***	**Honiball**	**1,425.00**
8184040199	**Computer Privacy Annoyances, *218 Pages***	**Tynan**	**225.00**
8184041586	**Computer Security Basics, 2/ed, *324 Pages***	**Lehtinen**	**325.00**
8173660638	Creating Effective JavaHelp, *196 Pages*	Lewis	125.00
0596008589	**Creating Photomontages with Photoshop: A Designer's Notebook, *96 Pages***	**Collandre**	**800.00**
8184040180	**Creating WebSites: The Missing Manual, *559 Pages***	**MacDonald**	**400.00**
8173669163	CSS Cookbook (Cover CSS 2.1), *280 Pages*	Schmitt	275.00
8184042736	**CSS Cookbook 2/ed, *552 Pages***	**Schmitt**	**450.00**
8184042787	**CSS: The Definitive Guide 3/ed, *550* Pages**	**Meyer**	**500.00**
8184042000	**CSS: The Missing Manual, *494* Pages**	**McFarland**	**450.00**
8184042655	**CSS: Pocket Reference 2/ed, *142* Pages**	**Meyer**	**125.00**
8173667802	Database In Depth: The Relational Model for Practitioners, *250 Pgs*	C.J.Date	225.00
8173662363	Database Nation: The Death of Privacy in the 21st Century, *336 Pages*	Garfinkel	235.00
8173662894	Database Programming with JDBC & Java 2/ed, *348 Pages*	Reese	150.00
8173665664	Designing Embedded Hardware, *324 Pages*	Catsoulis	250.00
8184042590	**Designing Embedded Hardware 2/ed, *406 Pages***	**Catsoulis**	**275.00**
0596008031	**Designing Interfaces, *352 Pages***	**Tidwell**	**1,800.00**
8173662428	Developing Bio-informatics Computer Skills, *504 Pages*	Gibas	225.00
8173669473	Developing Feeds with RSS and Atom, *280 Pages*	Hammersley	300.00
8184040113	Digital Identity, *266 Pages*	Windley	275.00
0596005474	Digital Photography: Expert Techniques (Covers Photoshop CS), *496 Pages*	Milburn	1,375.00

ISBN	Title	Author	Price
0596006667	Digital Photography Hacks: 100 Industrial - Strength Tips & Tools, *336 Pages*	Story	800.00
0596100159	Digital Photography Pocket Guide, 3/ed, *160 Pages*	Story	450.00
0596008414	**Digital Photography: The Missing Manual, *432 Pages***	**Grover**	**1,200.00**
0596009461	Digital Video Hacks: Tips & Tools for Shooting, Editing & Sharing, *426 Pages*	Paul	800.00
0596005237	Digital Video Pocket Guide, *474 Pages*	Story	500.00
8173665672	DNS & BIND Cookbook, *248 Pages*	Liu	250.00
8184041969	**DNS & BIND (Covers BIND 9.3), 5/ed, *654 Pages***	**Albitz**	**500.00**
8173663785	DNS on Windows 2000, 2/ed, *376 Pages*	Larson	275.00
8173660506	DNS on Windows NT, *352 Pages*	Albitz	195.00
8184041039	**Dreamweaver 8: The Missing Manual, *964 Pages***	**David**	**600.00**
8184041209	**Dreawweaver 8 Design and Construction, *330 Pages***	**Campbell**	**375.00**
8173662991	Dreamweaver MX: The Missing Manual, *750 Pages*	McFarland	600.00
8173665281	Dynamic HTML: The Definitive Reference, 2/ed, *1,428 Pages*	Goodman	650.00
8184042779	**Dynamic HTML: The Definitive Reference, 3/ed, *1,336 Pages***	**Goodman**	**800.00**
8173669015	Eclipse (Coverage of 3.0), *344 Pages*	Holzner	325.00
8173669309	Eclipse Cookbook (Cover 3.0), *372 Pages*	Holzner	350.00
8173669945	Eclipse IDE Pocket Guide, *140 Pages*	Burnette	125.00
8173663017	Effective awk Programming, 3/ed, *454 Pages*	Robbins	325.00
8173667268	Enterprise JavaBeans (Covers EJB 2.1 & EJB 2.0 Includes workbook for JBoss 4.0), 4/ed, *798 Pages*	Monson - Haefel	500.00
8184041195	**Enterprise JavaBeans 3.0, 5/ed, *774 Pages***	**Monson-Haefel**	**500.00**
8173668167	Enterprise Service Architecture - O'Reilly SAP Series, *236 Pages*	Woods	225.00
8173666784	Enterprise Service Bus, *284 Pages*	Chappell	300.00
8184041446	**Enterprise SOA, *466 Pages***	**Woods**	**375.00**
8173669317	Essential ActionScript 2.0, *528 Pages*	Moock	400.00
8184040105	Essential Business Process Modeling, *362 Pages*	Havey	350.00
8184042752	**Essential CVS 2/ed, *442 Pages***	**Vesperman**	**425.00**
818404092X	**Essential Microsoft Operation Manager, *400 Pages***	**Fox**	**350.00**
8184040245	Essentail PHP Security, *310 Pages*	Shiflett	125.00
8173669430	Essentail SharePoint, *338 Pages*	Webb	325.00
8184042825	**Essential SNMP 2/ed, *480 Pages***	**Mauro**	**400.00**
817366529X	Essential System Administration, 3/ed, *1,178 Pages*	Frisch	525.00
8173666644	Essential System Administration Pocket Reference, *152 Pages*	Frisch	125.00
8173660255	Essential Windows NT System Administration, *488 Pages*	Frisch	225.00
8173662495	Ethernet: The Definitive Guide, *528 Pages*	Spurgeon	300.00
8173669619	Excel 2003 Personal Trainer **(Book / CD-ROM)**, (2 Color book) *490 Pages*	CustomGuide	550.00
8173668299	Excel 2003 Programming: A Developer's Notebook, *330 Pages*	Webb	325.00
8184040288	**Excel 2003 for Starters: The Missing Manual, *408 Pages***	**MacDonald**	**275.00**
8184042558	**Excel 2007: The Missing Manual, *870 Pages***	**MacDonald**	**550.00**
8173668035	Excel: The Missing Manual, *802 Pages*	MacDonald	550.00
8184040849	**Excel Scientific and Engineering Cookbook, *442 Pages***	**Bourg**	**400.00**
8173665257	Exploring the JDS Linux Desktop **(Book / CD-ROM)**, *418 Pages*	Adelstein	400.00
8184042175	**Fedora Linux, *670 Pages***	**Tyler**	**500.00**
8184041365	**Flash 8 Cookbook, *548 Pages***	**Lott**	**400.00**
8184041047	**Flash 8 Project for Learning Animation and Interactivity (Book / CD-ROM), *372 Pages***	**Shupe**	**400.00**

ISBN	Title	Author	Price
8173667470	Flash Hacks: 100 Industrial Strength Tips & Tools, *504 Pages*	Bhangal	400.00
8173668590	Flash Out of the Box: A User-Centric Beginner's Guide to Flash **(Book / CD-ROM)**, *264 Pages*	Hoekman	300.00
8173667314	Flash Remoting MX: The Definitive Guide, *652 Pages*	Muck	550.00
0596002874	Free As In Freedom: Richard Stallman's Crusade for Free Software, *243 Pages*	Williams	750.00
8184040504	**FrontPage 2003: The Missing Manual, *446 Pages***	**Mantaro**	**400.00**
817366868X	GDB Pocket Reference, *78 Pages*	Robbins	75.00
8184040857	**Google Advertising Tools, *366 Pages***	**Davis**	**375.00**
817366949X	Google Hacks: Tips & Tools for Smarter Searching 2/ed, *496 Pages*	Calishain	350.00
8184040873	**Google Maps Hacks: Tips & Tools for Geographic Searching & Remixing, *366 Pages***	**Gibson**	**350.00**
8173667136	Google Pocket Guide, *144 Pages*	Calishain	125.00
818404285X	**Google: The Missing Manual 2/ed, *478 Pages***	**Milstein**	**425.00**
0596006624	Hackers & Painters: Big Ideas from the Computer Age, *272 Pages*	Graham	700.00
8173668256	Hardcore Java, *354 Pages*	Simmons	300.00
8173663424	Hardening Cisco Routers, *196 Pages*	Akin	150.00
8173668213	Hardware Hacking Projects for Geeks, *358 Pages*	Fullam	350.00
8173664668	Head First Design Patterns, *688 Pages*	Sierra	500.00
8173665265	Head First EJB: Passing the Sun Certified Business Component Developer Exam, *744 Pages*	Sierra	450.00
8184040822	**Head First HTML with CSS & XHTML, *694 Pages***	**Freeman**	**500.00**
8173666024	Head First Java (Covers Java 5.0) 2/ed, *730 Pages*	Sierra	450.00
8184042213	**Head First Object - Oriented Analysis & Design, *648 Pages***	**McLaughlin**	**425.00**
817366403X	Head First Servlets & JSP: Passing the Sun Certified Web Component Developer Exam, *666 Pages*	Sierra	600.00
8184041055	**Head Rush Ajax, *464 Pages***	**McLaughlin**	**375.00**
8173669341	Hibernate: A Developer's Notebook, *190 Pages*	Elliott	200.00
8173669260	High Performance Linux Cluster with OSCAR, Rocks, OpenMosix, and MPI, *380 Pages*	Sloan	350.00
8173669023	High Performance MySQL: Optimization, Backups, Replication & Load Balancing, *304 Pages*	Zawodny	300.00
8173663165	Home Hacking Projects for Geeks, *346 Pages*	Faulkner	325.00
8173669449	Home Networking Annoyances: How to Fix the Most Annoying Things About Your Home Network, *234 Pages*	Ivens	250.00
8184040202	Home Networking: The Missing Manual, *263 Pages*	Lowe	275.00
8173665141	HTML & XHTML: The Definitive Guide, 5/ed, *676 Pages*	Musciano	500.00
8184042140	**HTML & XHTML: The Definitive Guide, 6/ed, *692 Pages***	**Musciano**	**500.00**
8173664323	HTML Pocket Reference, 2/ed, *100 Pages*	Niederst	70.00
8184042698	**HTML & XHTML Pocket Reference, 3/ed, *118 Pages***	**Robbins**	**125.00**
0596008597	**Illustrations with Photoshop: A Designer's Notebook, *96 Pages***	**Rodarmor**	**775.00**
0596100485	**InDesign Production Cookbook, *224 Pages***	**Dabbs**	**1,200.00**
8173665109	Information Architecture for the World Wide Web, 2/ed, *492 Pages*	Rosenfeld	400.00
8184040385	Integrating Excel and Access, *232 Pages*	Schmalz	250.00
8184040997	**Intermediate Perl, *290 Pages***	**Schwartz**	**300.00**
8173669414	Internet Annoyances: How to Fix the Most Annoying Things about Going Online, *266 Pages*	Gralla	250.00
8173661057	Internet Core Protocols: The Definitive Guide **(Book / CD-ROM)**, *476 Pgs*	Hall	375.00
8184040156	Internet Forensics, *250 Pages*	Jones	275.00
8173660158	Internet in a Nutshell, *456 Pages*	Quercia	215.00

ISBN	Title	Author	Price
8184041810	**The Internet: The Missing Manual, *466 Pages***	**Biersdorfer**	**350.00**
8173663378	IP Routing, *244 Pages*	Malhotra	200.00
8184042817	**IPv6 Essentials 2/ed, *450 Pages***	**Hagen**	**450.00**
8173663025	IPv6 Network Administration, *316 Pages*	Murphy	325.00
8173667489	IRC Hack: 100 Industrial-Strength Tips & Tools, *442 Pages*	Mutton	400.00
8173667373	J2EE Design Patterns, *390 Pages*	Crawford	325.00
8173663432	J2ME in a Nutshell: A Desktop Quick Reference, *474 Pages*	Topley	400.00
8173669295	Jakarta Commons Cookbook, *412 Pages*	O'Brien	375.00
8173669481	Jakarta Struts Cookbook, *536 Pages*	Siggelkow	400.00
8173667144	Jakarta Struts Pocket Reference, *142 Pages*	Cavaness	125.00
8173664471	Java & SOAP, *286 Pages*	Englander	275.00
8173664498	Java & XML Data Binding, *224 Pages*	McLaughlin	225.00
817366367X	Java & XML, 2/ed, *534 Pages*	McLaughlin	450.00
8173663793	Java & XSLT, *534 Pages*	Burke	350.00
8173668477	Java 1.5 Tiger: A Developer's Notebook, *210 Pages*	McLaughlin	175.00
8173669368	Java Cookbook (Coverage of 1.5), 2/ed, *872 Pages*	Darwin	600.00
8173666679	Java Data Objects, *568 Pages*	Jordan	350.00
8173666660	Java Database Best Practices, *304 Pages*	Eckstein	275.00
8184042176	**Java Generics and Collections, *308 Pages***	**Naftalin**	**325.00**
817366577X	Java Enterprise Best Practices, *296 Pages*	Eckstein	275.00
8173662843	Java Examples in a Nutshell 2/ed, *592 Pages*	Flanagan	225.00
8184042876	**Java Enterprise in a Nutshell: 3/ed, *906 Pages***	**Farley**	**600.00**
8173668639	Java Examples in a Nutshell: A Tutorial Companion to Java in a Nutshell, 3/ed, *728 Pages*	Flanagan	400.00
8173666687	Java Extreme Programming Cookbook, *296 Pages*	Burke	225.00
8173664625	Java Enterprise in a Nutshell: A Desktop Quick Reference, 2/ed, *1,004 Pages*	Farley	100.00
817366434X	Java in a Nutshell: A Desktop Quick Reference, 4/ed, *1,000 Pages*	Flanagan	600.00
8184042663	**Java in a Nutshell 5/ed, *1,266 Pages***	**Flanagan**	**650.00**
8184041187	**Java I/O, 2/ed, *740 Pages***	**Harold**	**550.00**
8173664404	Java Management Extensions, *318 Pages*	Perry	275.00
8173663211	Java Message Service, *300 Pages*	Monson-Haefel	225.00
817366353X	Java Network Programming, 3/ed, *770 Pages*	Harold	500.00
8173665117	Java NIO, *308 Pages*	Hitchens	275.00
8173665788	Java Performance Tuning, 2/ed, *600 Pages*	Shirazi	450.00
8173663904	Java Programming with Oracle JDBC, *504 Pages*	Bales	300.00
8173663815	Java RMI, *578 Pages*	Grosso	400.00
8173664129	Java Security, 2/ed, *624 Pages*	Oaks	500.00
8173668221	Java Servlet & JSP Cookbook, *756 Pages*	Perry	500.00
8173662851	Java Servlet Programming 2/ed, *786 Pages*	Hunter	500.00
8173665680	Java Swing, 2/ed, *1,288 Pages*	Loy	750.00
8173665923	Java Threads (Covers J2SE 5.0), 3/ed, *368 Pages*	Oaks	300.00
8173663440	Java Web Services, *286 Pages*	Chappell	300.00
8173666695	Java Web Services in a Nutshell: A Desktop Quick Reference (Covers J2EE 1.4 & JWSDP), *696 Pages*	Topley	500.00
8173666709	JavaScript and DHTML Cookbook, *546 Pages*	Goodman	475.00
8184041942	**JavaScript: The Definitive Guide, 5/ed, *1,032 Pages***	**Flanagan**	**750.00**
8173669031	JavaServer Faces, *614 Pages*	Bergsten	450.00
8173665303	JavaServer Pages (Covers JSP 2.0 & JSTL 1.1), 3/ed, *762 Pages*	Bergsten	550.00

ISBN	Title	Author	Price
8173663831	JavaServer Pages Pocket Reference, *96 Pages*	Bergsten	65.00
8173669465	JBoss: A Developer's Notebook, *182 Pages*	Richards	200.00
8184040172	JBoss at Work: A Practical Guide, *318 Pages*	Marrs	325.00
8173666717	JDBC Pocket Reference, *160 Pages*	Bales	100.00
8173668604	JUnit Pocket Guide, *100 Pages*	Beck	100.00
8184041160	**JUNOS Cookbook, *682 Pages***	**Garrett**	**450.00**
059600768X	Just A Geek, *296 Pages*	Wheaton	700.00
817366515X	JXTA in a Nutshell: A Desktop Quick Reference, *422 Pages*	Oaks	225.00
8173665605	Kerberos: The Definitive Guide, *280 Pages*	Garman	275.00
8173669724	Killer Game Programming in Java, *986 Pages*	Davison	675.00
8184040261	Knoppix Pocket Reference, *104 Pages*	Rankin	100.00
8173666725	LDAP System Administration, *318 Pages*	Carter	300.00
8184042868	**Learning C# 2005 2/ed, *566 Pages***	**Libberty**	**450.00**
8173669635	Learning GNU Emacs, 3/ed, *544 Pages*	Cameron	450.00
8184040334	**Learning Java, 3/ed (Book / CD-ROM) (Cover J2SE 5.0), *986 Pgs***	**Niemeyer**	**650.00**
8184042159	**Learning JavaScript, *366 Pages***	**Powers**	**350.00**
8173663912	Learning Oracle PL/SQL (Covers Oracle9i), *452 Pages*	Pribyl	325.00
8184042671	**Learning MySQL, *632 Pages***	**Tahaghoghi**	**525.00**
8184040040	Learning Perl 4/ed, *316 Pages*	Schwartz	300.00
8173667322	Learning PHP 5, *378 Pages*	Sklar	350.00
8184041535	**Learning PHP and MySQL, *390 Pages***	**Davis**	**325.00**
8173667381	Learning Python (Covers Python 2.3), 2/ed, *630 Pages*	Lutz	525.00
8184040121	Learning SQL, *318 Pages*	Beaulieu	200.00
8173668051	Learning the Bash Shell, 3/ed, *362 Pages*	Newham	375.00
8173664447	Learning the Korn Shell, 2/ed, *438 Pages*	Rosenblett	325.00
8173664234	Learning the UNIX Operating System, 5/ed, *174 Pages*	Peek	125.00
8173660611	Learning the vi Editor 6/ed, *352 Pages*	Lamb	250.00
8173666741	Learning UML, *304 Pages*	Si Alhir	150.00
818404268X	**Learning UML 2.0, *300 Pages***	**Miles**	**275.00**
817366563X	Learning Visual Basic .NET, *326 Pages*	Liberty	250.00
8184040903	**Learning Web Design: A Beginner's Guide to HTML, Graphics and Beyond, 2/ed, *484 Pages (with 16 Color Pages)***	**Niederst**	**375.00**
8173669422	Learning Windows Server 2003, *682 Pages*	Hassell	525.00
817366062X	lex & yacc 2/ed, *392 Pages*	Levine	225.00
8184041438	**Linux Annoyances for Geeks, *516 Pages***	**Jang**	**400.00**
8173668442	Linux Cookbook, *590 Pages*	Schroder	450.00
8184040164	Linux Desktop Pocket Guide, *202 Pages*	Brickner	150.00
8173663602	Linux Device Drivers, 2/ed, *650 Pages*	Rubini	450.00
8173668493	**Linux Device Drivers (Covers Version 2.6.10 Linux Kernel), 3/ed, *646 Pages***	**Rubini**	**450.00**
8173669627	Linux in a Nutshell, 5/ed: A Desktop Quick Reference, *954 Pages*	Siever	500.00
8173669457	Linux in a Windows World, *504 Pages*	Smith	450.00
8173668507	Linux iptables Pocket Reference, *106 Pages*	Purdy	100.00
8184040318	**Linux Multimedia Hacks, *342 Pages***	**Rankin**	**350.00**
8173662541	Linux Network Administrator's Guide, 2/ed, *510 Pages*	Kirch	400.00
8173664544	Linux Network Administrator's Guide, 3/ed, *372 Pages*	Kirch	350.00
8173668647	Linux Pocket Guide, *212 Pages*	Barrett	150.00
8173667187	Linux Security Cookbook, *340 Pages*	Barrett	325.00

ISBN	Title	Author	Price
817366675X	Linux Server Hacks: 100 Industrial - Strength Tips & Tools, *240 Pages*	Flickenger	225.00
8184040512	**Linux Server Hacks: Volume 2, *490 Pages***	**Hagen**	**400.00**
8184042884	**Linux Server Security: 2/ed, *556 Pages***	**Bauer**	**450.00**
8173668434	Linux Unwired, *322 Pages*	Weeks	300.00
8184041780	**LPI Linux Certification in a Nutshell, 2/ed, *996 Pages***	**Pritchard**	**650.00**
817366465X	Managing & Using MySQL, 2/ed, *448 Pages*	Reese	325.00
8173662746	Managing IMAP, *412 Pages*	Mullet	200.00
8173660271	Managing IP Networks with Cisco Routers, *352 Pages*	Ballew	200.00
8173663610	Managing NFS & NIS, 2/ed, *518 Pages*	Stern	400.00
8173669589	Managing Projects with GNU Make, 3/ed, *310 Pages*	Mecklenburg	325.00
8173665230	Managing RAID on Linux, *268 Pages*	Vadala	275.00
8173668655	Managing Security with Snort & IDS Tools, *296 Pages*	Cox Ph.D.	300.00
8173662800	Managing the Windows 2000 Registry, *564 Pages*	Robicheaux	325.00
0596007035	Mapping Hacks: Tips & Tools for Electronic Cartography, *574 Pages*	Erle	900.00
8173661162	Mastering Algorithms with C **(Book / DISK)**, *572 Pages*	Loudon	400.00
8173664455	Mastering FreeBSD and OpenBSD Security, *472 Pages*	Korff	425.00
8173664617	Mastering Oracle SQL (Covers Oracle Database10g), 2/ed, *504 Pgs*	Mishra	400.00
8173666768	Mastering Perl for Bioinformatics, *406 Pages*	Tisdall	300.00
8173665087	Mastering Regular Expressions, 2/ed, *492 Pages*	Friedl	400.00
8173665702	Mastering Visual Studio .NET 2003, *420 Pages*	Flanders	375.00
8173667918	Maven: A Developer's Notebook, *232 Pages*	Massol	250.00
8184042183	**MCSE Core Elective Exams in a Nutshell, *602 Pages***	**Bhardwaj**	**500.00**
8184041551	**MCSE Core Required Exams in a Nutshell, 3/ed, *750 Pages***	**Stanek**	**450.00**
8184040520	**Monad, *218 Pages***	**Oakley**	**225.00**
8173667497	Mono: A Developer's Notebook, *312 Pages*	Dumbill	325.00
8173665648	MySQL Cookbook (Covers MySQL 4.0), *1,028 Pages*	DuBois	750.00
8184042809	**MySQL Cookbook 2ed, *990 Pages***	**DuBois**	**750.00**
817366806X	MySQL in a Nutshell, *358 Pages*	Dyer	325.00
8173666776	MySQL Pocket Reference, *94 Pages*	Reese	100.00
8184041403	**MySQL Stored Procedure Programming, *650 Pages***	**Harrison**	**450.00**
8173665249	NetBeans: The Definitive Guide, *662 Pages*	Boudreau	500.00
8173668809	Network Security Assessment, *398 Pages*	McNab	400.00
8173663521	Network Security Hacks: 100 Industrial-Strength Tips & Tools, *328 Pages*	Lockhart	325.00
8184042744	**Network Security Hacks 2/ed, *492 Pages***	**Lockhart**	**425.00**
8173668396	Network Security Tools: Writing, Hacking, and Modifying Security Tools , *350 Pgs*	Dhanjani	350.00
8173663688	Network Troubleshooting Tools, *370 Pages*	Sloan	250.00
8173667926	Nokia Smartphone Hacks: Tips & Tools for Your Smallest Computer, *418 Pages*	Yuan	400.00
8173667845	NUnit Pocket Reference, *100 Pages*	Hamilton	100.00
8173668264	Office 2003 XML, *596 Pages*	Lenz	450.00
8184040296	Open Sources 2.0, *488 Pages*	DiBona	425.00
8173667721	Open Source for the Enterprise, *246 Pages*	Woods	250.00
8173667519	OpenOffice.org Writer **(Book / CD-ROM)**, *234 Pages*	Weber	250.00
8173667403	Optimizing Oracle Performance, *426 Pages*	Milsap	375.00
8173669287	Oracle Applications Server 10g Essentials, *292 Pages*	Greenwald	275.00
8173661170	Oracle Built-in Packages **(Book / DISK)**, *956 Pages*	Feuerstein	475.00

ISBN	Title	Author	Price
8173667071	Oracle Data Dictionary Pocket Reference, *150 Pages*	Kreines	125.00
8173660670	Oracle Database Administration: The Essential Reference, *552 Pgs*	Kreines	325.00
817366417X	Oracle DBA Checklist Pocket Reference, *88 Pages*	RevealNet	65.00
8184040008	Oracle DBA Pocket Guide, *164 Pages*	Kreines	125.00
8173660689	Oracle Distributed Systems **(Book / DISK)**, *552 Pages*	Dye	325.00
8173664110	Oracle Essentials: Oracle9i, Oracle8i & Oracle8, 2/ed, *382 Pgs*	Greenwald	250.00
817366935X	Oracle Essentials: Oracle Database 10g, 3/ed, *368 Pages*	Greenwald	275.00
817366580X	Oracle in a Nutshell: A Desktop Quick Reference, *934 Pages*	Greenwald	600.00
8173664560	Oracle Initialization Parameters Pocket Reference (Oracle Database 10g), *128 Pages*	Kreines	125.00
8173663629	Oracle PL/SQL Best Practices, *208 Pages*	Feuerstein	200.00
8173661189	Oracle PL/SQL Built-ins Pocket Reference, *78 Pages*	Feuerstein	60.00
8184040350	Oracle PL/SQL for DBAs, *466 Pages*	Feuerstein	350.00
818404254X	**Oracle PL/SQL Language Pocket Reference 2/ed, *140 Pgs***	**Feuerstein**	**125.00**
8184040482	**Oracle PL/SQL Programming, 4/ed, *1,210 Pages***	**Feuerstein**	**600.00**
8173662401	Oracle PL/SQL Programming: A Developer's Workbook, *576 Pgs*	Feuerstein	300.00
8173661197	Oracle PL/SQL Programming: Guide to Oracle8i Features **(Book / DISK)**, *264 Pages*	Feuerstein	235.00
8173668116	Oracle Regular Expression Pocket Reference, *74 Pages*	Burcham	75.00
8173661200	Oracle SAP Administration, *208 Pages*	Burleson	175.00
8173660298	Oracle Scripts **(Book / CD-ROM)**, *208 Pages*	Lomansky	250.00
8173660719	Oracle Security, *448 Pages*	Theriault	220.00
8173663637	Oracle SQL* Loader: The Definitive Guide, *278 Pages*	Gennick	175.00
8173669333	Oracle SQL*Plus Pocket Reference, 3/ed, *160 Pages*	Gennick	125.00
8173666067	Oracle SQL*Plus: The Definitive Guide, 2/ed, *592 Pages*	Gennick	400.00
8173662916	Oracle SQL: The Essential Reference, *424 Pages*	Kreines	200.00
8173661847	Oracle Utilities Pocket Reference, *136 Pages*	Mishra	100.00
8173661219	Oracle Web Applications: PL/SQL Developer's Intro, *264 Pages*	Odewahn	180.00
817366028X	Oracle8 Design Tips, *136 Pages*	Ensor	120.00
8173668027	PC Annoyances: How to Fix the Most Annoying Thingsabout your Personal Computer, *236 Pages*	Bass	225.00
8184042523	**PC Annoyances 2/ed : How to Fix the Most Annoying Thingsabout your Personal Computer, *266 Pages***	**Bass**	**300.00**
8173667152	PC Hacks: 100 Industrial-Strength Tips & Tools, *316 Pages*	Aspinwall	300.00
8173669732	PC Hardware Annoyances: How to Fix the Most ANNOYING Things About Your Computer Hardware, *276 Pages*	Bigelow	275.00
817366532X	PC Hardware in a Nutshell: A Desktop Quick Reference, 3/ed, *848 Pages*	Thompson	325.00
8173668272	PC Pest Control, *296 Pages*	Gralla	300.00
818404139X	**PC's: The Missing Manual, *612 Pages***	**Rathbone**	**450.00**
8173667128	PDF Hacks: 100 Industrial-Strength Tips & Tools, *308 Pages*	Steward	300.00
8184042760	**Perl 6 and Parrot Essentials 2/ed, *304 Pages***	**Randal**	**325.00**
8173664463	Perl & XML, *224 Pages*	Ray	175.00
8173661073	Perl 5 Pocket Reference, 3/ed, *96 Pages*	Vromans	70.00
8173668280	Perl Best Practices, *554 Pages*	Conway	425.00
8173667330	Perl Cookbook, 2/ed, *976 Pages*	Christiansen	675.00
8184041381	**Perl Hacks, *310 Pages***	**Chromatic**	**325.00**
8173668043	Perl Template Toolkit, *600 Pages*	Chamberlain	525.00
8173668361	Perl Testing: A Developer's Notebook, *212 Pages*	Langworth	225.00
8173665710	PHP Cookbook, *638 Pages*	Sklar	550.00

ISBN	Title	Author	Price
8184040814	**PHP Hacks: Tips & Tools for Creating Dynamic Web Sites, *468 Pages***	**Herrington**	**400.00**
8184040237	PHP in a Nutshell, *370 Pages*	Hudson	325.00
8184040253	PHPUnit Pocket Guide, *88 Pages*	Bergmann	100.00
0596008600	**Photo Retouching with Photoshop: A Designer's Notebook, *96 Pgs***	**CLEC'H**	**775.00**
0596100205	**Photoshop Blending Modes Cookbook for Digital Photographers, *176 Pages***	**Beardsworth**	**1,025.00**
0596008511	**Photoshop CS2 Raw: Using Adobe Camera Raw, Bridge, and Photoshop to Get the Most Out of Your Digital Camera, *206 Pages***	**Aaland**	**1,075.00**
0596100213	**Photoshop Filter Effects Encyclopedia, *176 Pages***	**Pring**	**1,050.00**
0596100620	**Photoshop Fine Art Effects Cookbook, *176 Pages***	**Beardsworth**	**1,050.00**
0596100221	**Photoshop Photo Effects Cookbook, *176 Pages***	**Shelbourne**	**1,025.00**
0596100302	**Photoshop Retouching Cookbook for Digital Photographers, *176 Pages***	**Huggins**	**1,025.00**
817366871X	Postfix: The Definitive Guide, *288 Pages*	Dent	275.00
8173669805	Powerpoint 2003 Personal Trainer **(Book / CD-ROM)**, (2 Color book) *242 Pages*	CustomGuide	425.00
8184042566	**PowerPoint 2007: The Missing Manual, *502 Pages***	**Veer**	**450.00**
8173660301	Practical C Programming 3/ed, *456 Pages*	Oualline	225.00
8173666822	Practical C++ Programming, 2/ed, *582 Pages*	Oualline	225.00
8184040059	Practical Development Environments, *340 Pages*	Doar	325.00
817366711X	Practical mod_perl, *932 Pages*	Bekman	675.00
8184040326	**Practical Perforce, *370 Pages***	**Wingerd**	**375.00**
8173663920	Practical PostgreSQL **(Book / CD-ROM)**, *642 Pages*	Command Prompt Inc.	450.00
8173666733	Practical RDF, *360 Pages*	Powers	325.00
8173666830	Practical Unix & Internet Security, 3/ed, *994 Pages*	Garfinkel	650.00
8173664390	Practical VoIP Using VOCAL, *532 Pages*	Dang	450.00
8184040091	Prefactoring, *248 Pages*	Pugh	250.00
8184042108	**Process Improvement Essentials, *364 Pages***	**Persse, PhD**	**400.00**
8184040229	Producing Open Sources Software, *302 Pages*	Fogel	325.00
8184040342	**Programming .NET Components, 2/ed (Covers .NET 2.0 & Visual Studio 2005), *656 Pages***	**Lowy**	**425.00**
8173667209	Programming .NET Security, *704 Pages*	Freeman	550.00
8173664382	Programming .NET Web Services, *500 Pages*	Ferrara	375.00
8173667411	Programming .NET Windows Applications (Covers .NET 1.1, & Visual Studio .NET 2003), *1,316 Pages*	Liberty	750.00
8184042086	**Programming Atlas, *418 Pages***	**Wenz**	**375.00**
8184040970	**Programming ASP.NET (Covers 2.0), 3/ed, *966 Pages***	**Liberty**	**600.00**
8173669651	**Programming C# (Covers C# 2.0, .NET 2.0 & Visual Studio 2005), 4/ed, *680 Pages***	**Liberty**	**525.00**
817366076X	Programming Embedded Systems in C & C++, *198 Pages*	Barr	150.00
8184042620	**Programming Embedded Systems 2/ed: with C and GNU Development Tools, *340 Pages***	**Barr**	**250.00**
8184041454	**Programming Excel with VBA and .NET, *1,128 Pages***	**Webb**	**750.00**
8173669694	Programming Flash Communication Server, *842 Pages*	Lesser	600.00
8173661278	Programming Internet E-mail, *384 Pages*	Wood	225.00
8173668183	Programming Jakarta Struts 2/ed, *470 Pages*	Cavaness	400.00
8184040792	**Programming MapPoint in .NET (Book / CD-ROM), *400 Pages***	**Thota**	**350.00**

ISBN	Title	Author	Price
8173662657	Programming Perl 3/ed, *1,116 Pages*	Wall	750.00
8173663114	Programming PHP, *530 Pages*	Lerdorf	350.00
818404271X	**Programming PHP 2/ed, *564 Pages***	**Lerdorf**	**425.00**
8173667500	Programming Python (Covers Python 2) **(Book / CD-ROM)**, 2/ed, *1,305 Pages*	Lutzf	750.00
8173667861	**Programming SQL Server 2005, *600 Pages***	**Wildermuth**	**400.00**
8173662371	Programming the Perl DBI, *372 Pages*	Descartes	200.00
8173667063	Programming Visual Basic .NET 2003, 2/ed, *564 Pages*	Liberty	425.00
8184040377	**Programming Visual Basic 2005, *580 Pages***	**Liberty**	**400.00**
8173665737	Programming Web Services with Perl, *492 Pages*	Ray	400.00
8173662045	Programming Web Services with SOAP, *268 Pages*	Snell	200.00
817366207X	Programming Web Services with XML-RPC, *240 Pages*	St.Laurent	175.00
0596101139	**Programming Windows Presentation Foundation, *430 Pages***	**Sells**	**1,100.00**
8173668175	Programming with QT (Covers Qt 3), 2/ed, *532 Pages*	Dalheimer	450.00
8184041500	**Project 2003 Personal Trainer, (Book / CD-ROM), *246 Pages***	**CustomGuide**	**300.00**
817366479X	Python Cookbook (Covers Python 2.3 & 2.4), 2/ed, *852 Pages*	Martelli	600.00
8173666857	Python in a Nutshell: A Desktop Quick Reference (Cover Python 2.2), *662 Pages*	Martelli	500.00
8173669708	Python Pocket Reference (Covers Python 2.4), 3/ed, *168 Pages*	Lutz	125.00
8173668485	qmail, *268 Pages*	Levine	275.00
817366689X	Real World Web Services, *230 Pages*	Iverson	225.00
8184041985	**The Relational Database Dictionary, *126 Pages***	**Date**	**150.00**
8173667276	Regular Expression Pocket Reference, *112 Pages*	Stubblebine	100.00
8184041373	**Repairing and Upgrading Your PC, *462 Pages***	**Thompson**	**350.00**
8184041802	**Ruby Cookbook, *920 Pages***	**Carlson**	**650.00**
8184041993	**Ruby on Rails: Up and Running, *196 Pages***	**Tate**	**225.00**
0596007191	Revolution in the Valley, *324 Pages*	Hertzfeld	775.00
8184040865	**RFID Essentials, *276 Pages***	**Glover**	**275.00**
8173669686	RT Essentials, *228 Pages*	Vincent	250.00
8173665206	Running Linux, 4/ed, *702 Pages*	Welsh	425.00
8184042728	**Running Linux, 5/ed, *986 Pages***	**Welsh**	**600.00**
8173667055	Samba Pocket Reference, 2/ed, *146 Pages*	Eckstein	125.00
8173664226	SAX2 (Simple API for XML), *248 Pages*	Brownell	175.00
8173667217	Secure Coding: Principles & Practices, *200 Pages*	Graff	225.00
8173667284	Secure Programming Cookbook for C and C++, *800 Pages*	Viega	600.00
8173663262	Securing Windows NT/2000 Servers for the Internet, *200 Pages*	Norberg	125.00
8173669376	Securing Windows Server 2003, *456 Pages*	Danseglio	400.00
8184040083	Security and Usability, *748 Pages*	Cranor	550.00
817366840X	Security Warrior, *562 Pages*	Peikari	500.00
8173660786	sed & awk, 2/ed, *440 Pages*	Dougherty	300.00
817366918X	SELINUX NSA's Open Source Security Enhanced Linux, *264 Pgs*	McCarty	275.00
8173665834	sendmail, 3/ed, *1,238 Pages*	Costales	850.00
817366823X	sendmail Cookbook, *418 Pages*	Hunt	400.00
8173666865	Sequence Analysis in a Nutshell: A Guide to Common Tools and Databases (Covers EMBOSS 2.5.0), *310 Pages*	Markel	275.00
817366983X	SharePoint Office Pocket Guide, *94 Pages*	Webb	100.00
817366739X	SharePoint User's Guide, *158 Pages*	IDC	150.00
8184040679	**Skype Hacks: Tips & Tools for Cheap, Fun, Innovative Phone Service, *354 Pages***	**Sheppard**	**350.00**

ISBN	Title	Author	Price
8173669503	Snort Cookbook, *296 Pages*	Orebaugh	300.00
8173669198	SpamAssassin (Covers 3.0), *232 Pages*	Schwartz	250.00
8173668191	Spidering Hacks: 100 Industrial - Strength Tips & Tools, *436 Pgs*	Hemenway	350.00
817366837X	Spring: A Developer's Notebook, *202 Pages*	Tate	200.00
8184040687	**SQL Cookbook, *640 Pages***	**Molinaro**	**475.00**
8184042205	**SQL Hacks, *424 Pages***	**Cumming**	**400.00**
8173666520	SQL in a Nutshell (Covers SQL Server, DB2, MySQL, Oracle & PostgreSQL), 2/ed, *720 Pages*	Kline	450.00
8173667438	SQL Pocket Reference (Cover Oracle. DB2, SQL Server & MySQL), *170 Pages*	Gennick	125.00
8173668248	SQL Tunning (Covers Oracle, DB2 & SQL Server), *356 Pages*	Tow	325.00
8173668418	Squid: The Definitive Guide, *472 Pages*	Wessels	450.00
8184042795	**SSH: The Secure Shell: The Definitive Guide 2/ed, *680 Pages***	**Barrett**	**525.00**
8173668574	STL Pocket Reference, *136 Pages*	Lischner	100.00
8184042639	**Statistics Hacks, *380 Pages***	**Frey**	**350.00**
8184041799	**SUSE Linux, *460 Pages***	**Brown**	**400.00**
8173664811	Swing Hacks, *554 Pages*	Marinacci	425.00
8173665311	Switching to VoIP, *514 Pages*	Wallingford	450.00
8173669511	SWT: A Developer's Notebook, *330 Pages*	Hatton	325.00
8173663254	T1: A Survival Guide, *312 Pages*	Gast	225.00
8184040539	**Talk is Cheap: Switching to Internet Telephones, *278 Pages***	**Gaskin**	**275.00**
817366093X	Tcl/Tk in a Nutshell: A Desktop Quick Reference, *480 Pages*	Raines	240.00
8173664676	TCP/IP Network Administration 3/ed, *756 Pages*	Hunt	500.00
8173666512	Test Driving Linux: From Windows to Linux in 60 Seconds **(Book / CD-ROM)**, *372 Pages*	Brickner	350.00
818404030X	**Time Management for System Administrators, *238 Pages***	**Limoncelli**	**250.00**
8173666032	**TOAD Pocket Reference for Oracle, 2/ed, *136 Pages***	**McGrath**	**125.00**
8173666873	Tomcat: The Definitive Guide (Cover Tomcat 4), *336 Pages*	Brittain	300.00
8184040210	Twisted Network Programming Essentials, *210 Pages*	Fettig	275.00
8184041594	**Ubuntu Hacks, *462 Pages***	**Oxer**	**350.00**
8184040024	UML 2.0 in a Nutshell, *246 Pages*	Pilone	200.00
8173667225	UML Pocket Reference, *96 Pages*	Pilone	100.00
8184040768	**Understanding Linux Network Internals, *1,074 Pages***	**Benvenuti**	**600.00**
8184040830	**Understanding the Linux Kernel (Cov Version 2.6), 3/ed, *954 Pages***	**Bovet**	**550.00**
8184041608	**Unicode Explained, *692 Pages***	**Korpela**	**525.00**
817366627X	Unit Test Frameworks **(Book / CD-ROM)**, *222 Pages*	Hamill	225.00
8184040601	**Unix in a Nutshell, 4/ed, *992 Pages***	**Robbins**	**450.00**
8173665656	Unix Power Tools, 3/ed, *1,162 Pages*	Powers	750.00
8173666202	Upgrading to PHP 5 (Covers MySQL 4.1), *358 Pages*	Trachtenberg	350.00
8173660948	Using & Managing PPP, *464 Pages*	Sun	240.00
8173665842	Using Samba, 2/ed, *570 Pages*	Eckstein	500.00
817366594X	VB .NET Language Pocket Reference, *160 Pages*	Roman	125.00
8173666881	VBScript in a Nutshell: A Desktop Quick Reference, 2/e, *528 Pages*	Lomax	400.00
8173663300	VBScript Pocket Reference, *118 Pages*	Childs	60.00
8173668582	Version Control With Subversion, *332 Pages*	Collins - Sussman	350.00
8173662622	vi Editor Pocket Reference, *76 Pages*	Robbins	60.00
8173661340	Virtual Private Networks, 2/ed, *228 Pages*	Scott	150.00
8173666164	**Visual Basic 2005: A Developer's Notebook, *272 Pages***	**MacDonald**	**250.00**
8184040911	**Visual Basic 2005 in a Nutshell 3/ed, *766 Pages***	**Patrick**	**500.00**

ISBN	Title	Author	Price
8184040067	**Visual Basic 2005 Jumpstart, *226 Pages***	**Lee**	**225.00**
8173669740	**Visual C# 2005: A Developer's Notebook, *250 Pages***	**Libberty**	**225.00**
8184042094	**Visual Basic 2005 Cookbook, *754 Pages***	**Craig**	**575.00**
8173660964	Visual Basic Controls in a Nutshell, *512 Pages*	Dictor	310.00
8184040695	**VOIP Hacks: Tips & Tools for Internet Telephony, *326 Pages***	**Wallingford**	**325.00**
0596007337	We the Media: Grassroots Journalism by the People,for the People, *320 Pages*	Gillmor	775.00
8173669058	Web Database Application with PHP & MySQL (Covers PEAR, PHP 5 & MySQL 4.1), 2/ed, *828 Pages*	Willaims	600.00
8173663750	Web Design in a Nutshell: A Desktop Quick Reference, 2/ed, *656 Pages*	Niederst	425.00
8184040989	Web Design in a Nutshell: A Desktop Quick Reference, 3/ed, *828 Pages*	Niederst	450.00
8173664412	Web Performance Tuning, 2/ed, *488 Pages*	Killelea	350.00
8173665214	Web Privacy with P3P, *350 Pages*	Cranor	300.00
8173663947	Web Security, Privacy & Commerce, 2/ed, *768 Pages*	Garfinkel	500.00
8173667624	**Web Site Cookbook, *290 Pages***	**Addison**	**300.00**
8173663394	Web Services Essentials, *320 Pages*	Cerami	200.00
8173669678	Web Site Measurement Hacks: Tips & Tools to Help Optimize Your Online Business, *442 Pages*	Peterson	400.00
8173663092	WebLogic 8.1: The Definitive Guide, *860 Pages*	Mountjoy	600.00
8173661308	The Whole Internet: The Next Generation, *576 Pages*	Conner/Krol	425.00
8173661367	Win32 API Programming with Visual Basic **(Book / CD-ROM)**, *534 Pgs*	Roman	400.00
8173663319	Windows 2000 Commands Pocket Reference, *122 Pages*	Frisch	60.00
8184042604	**Windows Developers Power Tools, *1,322 Pages***	**Avery**	**750.00**
8173660883	Windows NT TCP/IP Network Administration, *512 Pages*	Hunt	250.00
0596100833	**Windows Seat, *152 Pages***	**Kost**	**1,600.00**
8184040776	**Windows Server 2003 Security Cookbook, *522 Pages***	**Danseglio**	**475.00**
8173668833	Windows Server Hacks: 100 Industrial-Strength Tips & Tools , *328 Pages*	Tulloch	325.00
8184042582	**Windows Vista: The Missing Manual, *860 Pages***	**Pogue**	**600.00**
817366966X	Windows XP Cookbook, *690 Pages*	Allen	500.00
8173667454	Windows XP Hacks: 100 Industrial-Strength Tips & Tools, *294 Pages*	Gralla	350.00
8173669643	Windows XP Personal Trainer **(Book / CD-ROM)**, *480 Pages*	CustomGuide	550.00
8173666911	Windows XP Pocket Reference, *196 Pages*	Karp	125.00
8173667462	Wireless Hacks: 100 Industrial-Strength Tips & Tools, *424 Pages*	Flickenger	275.00
817366692X	Word Pocket Guide, *160 Pages*	Glenn	125.00
8173665354	Writing Excel Macros with VBA, 2/ed, *580 Pages*	Roman	450.00
8173660778	Writing Word Macros, *416 Pages*	Roman	275.00
818404142X	**XAML in a Nutshell, *316 Pages***	**MacVittie**	**300.00**
8173668310	X Windows Reference Manaul (3 Volume Set)	Nye	1,350.00
8173666156	XML Hacks: 100 Industrial-Strength Tips & Tools, *490 Pages*	Fitzgerald	425.00
8173668450	XML in a Nutshell (Covers XML 1.1 & XInclude), 3/ed, *724 Pages*	Harold	500.00
8173663343	XML Pocket Reference, 2/ed, *128 Pages*	Eckstein	100.00
8184042647	**XML Pocket Reference, 3/ed, *198 Pages***	**St. Laurent**	**125.00**
8173664900	XSLT 1.0 Pocket Reference, *188 Pages*	Lenz	150.00
8184040784	**XSLT Cookbook (Cover XSLT 1.0 & 2.0, 2/ed, *786 Pages***	**Mangano**	**500.00**
8184040075	Yahoo! Hacks: Tips & Tools for Living on the Web Frontier, *504 Pgs*	Bausch	400.00
8184040881	**Zero Configuration Networking: The Definitive Guide, *252 Pages***	**Cheshire**	**275.00**

ISBN	Title	Author	Price

FORTHCOMING TITLES

January 2007

0596100310	Digital Video Production Cookbook, *192 Pages*	Kenworthy	1,200.00
8184043171	Flash 8: The Missing Manual, *460 Pages*	Moore	500.00
8184043198	Information Dashboard Design, *223 Pages*	Few	250.00
818404321X	Learning SQL on SQL Server 2005, *342 Pages*	Bagui	350.00
0596101686	Photoshop Workflow Setups, *207 Pages*	Tapp	1,170.00
0596527683	Practical Color Management: Eddie Tapp on Digital Photography, *168 Pages*	Tapp	1,170.00
059652370X	Stephen Johnson on Digital Photography, *320 Pages*	Johnson	1,500.00

February 2007

8184043244	Fonts & Encodings, *992 Pages*	Haralambous	675.00
8184043309	BacKup & Recovery, *729 Pages*	Preston	675.00
8184043317	Rail Cookbook, *600 Pages*	Orsini	550.00

March 2007

8184043333	Ajax on Java, *176 Pages*	Olson	200.00
8184043341	Bash Cookbook, *600 Pages*	Newham	575.00
818404335X	Linux Kernal in a Nutshell, *352 Pages*	Kroah-Hartman	375.00
8184043368	Windows Vista Annoyances for Geeks, *704 Pages*	Karp	675.00
8184043376	Windows Vista for Starters: The Missing Manual, *400 Pages*	Pogue	375.00

April 2007

8184043384	A+, Network+, Security+ Exams in a Nutshell, *752 Pages*	Bhardwaj	675.00
8184043392	Access Data Analysis Cookbook, *400 Pages*	Bluttman	375.00
8184043406	Head First PMP, *600 Pages*	Stellman	575.00
8184043414	Learning WCF, *456 Pages*	Bustamante	400.00
8184043422	Progamming Flex 2, *528 Pages*	Kazoun	500.00
8184043430	Progamming WCF Services, *600 Pages*	L&oumlwy	600.00
8184043449	Understanding MySQL Internals, *504 Pages*	Pachey	500.00
8184043457	Windows Vista: The Definitive Guide, *856 Pages*	Stanek	675.00
8184043465	XQuery, *600 Pages*	Walmsley	575.00

May 2007

8184043473	Adobe Photoshop Lightroom Adventure, *304 Pages*	Aaland	300.00
8184043481	Asterisk Cookbook, *504 Pages*	Meggelen	575.00
818404349X	Developing Databases with Access, *504 Pages*	Freeze	495.00
8184043503	Head First Algebra, *664 Pages*	Davis	500.00
8184043511	Head First Web Design, *600 Pages*	Barr	575.00
818404352X	Linux System Administration, *600 Pages*	Thompson	595.00
8184043538	Linux System Programming, *456 Pages*	Love	400.00
8184043546	Ruby in a Nutshell, 2/ed, *304 Pages*	Matsumoto	300.00
8184043554	XSLT, 2/ed, *800 Pages*	Tidwell	675.00

- **Dates & Prices of forthcoming titles are tentative and subject to change without notice.**
- **All Prices are in Indian Rupees**
- **TITLES RELEASED AFTER January 2006 ARE MARKED IN BOLD.**